1 MONTH OF FREE READING

at

www.ForgottenBooks.com

By purchasing this book you are eligible for one month membership to ForgottenBooks.com, giving you unlimited access to our entire collection of over 1,000,000 titles via our web site and mobile apps.

To claim your free month visit:

www.forgottenbooks.com/free1112928

* Offer is valid for 45 days from date of purchase. Terms and conditions apply.

ISBN 978-0-331-36896-3
PIBN 11112928

This book is a reproduction of an important historical work. Forgotten Books uses state-of-the-art technology to digitally reconstruct the work, preserving the original format whilst repairing imperfections present in the aged copy. In rare cases, an imperfection in the original, such as a blemish or missing page, may be replicated in our edition. We do, however, repair the vast majority of imperfections successfully; any imperfections that remain are intentionally left to preserve the state of such historical works.

Forgotten Books is a registered trademark of FB &c Ltd.
Copyright © 2018 FB &c Ltd.
FB &c Ltd, Dalton House, 60 Windsor Avenue, London, SW19 2RR.
Company number 08720141. Registered in England and Wales.

For support please visit www.forgottenbooks.com

Historic, Archive Document

Do not assume content reflects current scientific knowledge, policies, or practices.

COTTON LITERATU
SELECTED REFERENCES

PREPARED IN THE LIBRARY OF THE UNITED STATES DEPARTMENT OF AGRICULTU
WITH THE COOPERATION OF THE BUREAU OF AGRICULTURAL ECONOMICS,
BUREAU OF PLANT INDUSTRY AND BUREAU OF ENTOMOLOGY
AND PLANT QUARANTINE

COMPILED BY EMILY L. DAY, LIBRARY SPECIALIST IN COTTON MARKETING,
BUREAU OF AGRICULTURAL ECONOMICS, WASHINGTON, D. C.

Vol. 7　　　　　　　　April, 1937　　　　　　　　No. 4

CONTENTS

Production	127
General	127
Botany	129
Agronomy	129
Diseases	134
Insects	135
Farm Engineering	138
Farm Management	140
Farm Social Problems	140
Cooperation in Production	141
Preparation	142
General	142
Ginning	142
Baling	143
Marketing	143
General	143
Demand and Competition	145
Supply and Movement	154
Prices	158
Marketing and Handling Methods and Practices	159
Services and Facilities	160
Marketing Costs	162
Cooperation in Marketing	162
Utilization	164
General	164
Fiber, Yarn, and Fabric Quality	165
Technology of Manufacture	172
Technology of Consumption	174
Cottonseed and Cottonseed Products	176
Legislation, Regulation, and Adjudication	177

COTTON LITERATURE is compiled mainly from material received in the Library of the U. S. Department of Agriculture.

Copies of the publications listed herein can not be supplied by the Department except in the case of publications expressly designated as issued by the U. S. Department of Agriculture. Books, pamphlets, and periodicals mentioned may ordinarily be obtained from their respective publishers or from the Secretary of the issuing organization. Many of them are available for consultation in public or other libraries.

C O T T O N L I T E R A T U R E
April, 1937

PRODUCTION

General

American phytopathological society. Abstracts of papers accepted for presentation at the 28th annual meeting...Atlantic City, New Jersey, December 28 to 31, 1936. Phytopathology 27(2):122-123,136,137,143, February 1937. (Published at Lime & Green Sts., Lancaster, Pa.) 464.8 P56
    A comparison of linted and acid-delinted cotton seed, by J.G. Brown, pp.122-123; A disorder of cotton plants recently observed in Louisiana, by D.C. Neal, p.136; Blue stain of cotton is due to a fungus, by O.P. Owens, p.137; Penetration and invasion of phymatotrichum omnivorum in cotton roots grown under pure-culture conditions, by G.M. Watkins, p.143.

Association of economic biologists, Coimbatore. Proceedings...volume III. 1935. 61pp., illus., tables, charts. Coimbatore, 1936. 442.9 As7
    Partial contents: Intercultivation of rain-fed cottons in the Madras Presidency, by V. Ramanatha Ayyar, pp.1-5; Stenosis in Gujarat cotton, by V.N. Likhite, pp.15-17; Host range of the Gujarat cotton root-rot, by V.N. Likhite, pp.18-20; The nature of resistance in cotton plants to stem-weevil, by K. Dharma Rajulu, pp.21-31.
    References at end of each article.

Chavarria A., Carlos. Preparación de tierras para el cultivo del algodón. Boletin de Agricultura y Trabajo [Nicaragua] 7(59/60): 25-26. July/August 1935. (Published at Managua, D.N., Nicaragua). 8 N51
    Preparation of land for the cultivation of cotton.
    Cotton insects are also described.

Georgia Coastal plain experiment station. Sixteenth annual report, 1935-1936; crop yields shown for calendar year 1935. Ga. Coastal

Plain Expt. Sta., Bull. 26, 106pp., illus., tables. Tifton. 1936.   100 G292
   Cotton, pp.11-17; Cotton insect investigations, p.61.

India. Burma. Department of agriculture. Report on the operations...for the year ended the 31st March 1936. 180pp., tables. Rangoon, 1936. . 22 B92Re
   Partial contents: Annual administration report of the Myingyan Circle for the year ending the 31st March 1936--Cotton, pp.159-160; Cotton, pp.169-170.

India. Madras présidency. Department of agriculture.   Reports of subordinate officers... for 1935-36. 165pp., tables.   Madras, 1936. 22 M26Re
   Partial contents: Administration report of the cotton specialist for the year 1935-36, pp.106-111.

India. United provinces.   Triennial report of experiments carried out on the various agricultural stations during the years 1932-33, 1933-34 and 1934-35. 114pp. Allahabad, Supt. printing and stationery, United Provinces, 1936.   107.5 In22R
   Cotton variety trials, pp.51-53; Control of insect pests...pests of cotton--(pink boll-worm), p.108.

Kenya. Department of agriculture. Annual report, 1935. Vol.II, 164pp.   Nairobi, 1936. 24 Af8A
   Cotton in various provinces, pp.87-88, 94-97, 112-116.

Uganda protectorate. Department of agriculture. Annual report...for the year ended 30th June 1936, (Part II). 123pp., tables, charts. Entebbe, Government printer, 1936.   24 Ug12
   Partial contents: Jassids, pp.12-15; Cotton stainers, pp.15-16; Lygus, pp.16-17; Helopeltis p.18; Report on a year's investigation of Platyedra gossypiella (Pink boll worm) in Uganda, by T.H.C. Taylor, pp.19-33; Cotton wilt disease, pp.40-42; Botanical work, Bukalasa--Cotton, pp.69-79; and Botanical work, Serere--Cotton, pp.81-91.

Botany

    Krug, H.P. Effeito de faiscas electricas (raios) sobre algodoeiros. Revista de Agricultura (Piracicaba) 11(11/12):487-490, illus. November/December 1936. (Published at Caixo Postal 60, Piracicaba, Estado de Sao Paulo, Brazil) 9.2 R324
      English summary.
      Effect of electric flashes (rays of light) on cotton plants.

    Rigler, J. von. Kann das reifen der kapseln der baumwolle-pflanze durch beringeln und beschneiden beschleunigt werden? Kiserletügyi Közlemenyek 39(4/6):129-140, illus., tables, charts. July/December 1936. (Published at Budapest, Hungary) 105.9 H89
      In Hungarian. Summary in German.
      Can the ripening of the cotton boll be hastened by ringing and topping?

Agronomy

    Algunas caracteristiscas de las variedades de algodón que se han cultivado en estado experimental. Gaceta Algodonera 12(156):5. Jan.31,1937. (Published at Reconquista 331, Casilla Correo 550, Buenos Aires, Argentina) 72.8 G11
      Some characteristics of the cotton varieties that are cultivated at the experiment stations [in Argentina].

    Brown, J. G. Seed delinting question. Practice advocated for cotton disease control and other advantages. Ariz. Producer 15(25):21,24. Mar.15,1937. (Published at 313 No. 3rd Ave., Phoenix, Ariz.) 6 Ar44
      "Good cotton seed, the proper time to plant, and the best possible seed-bed constitute three factors which the successful cotton grower heeds."

    Collins, Emerson R. Investigations on the mechanical application of fertilizers for cotton in North Carolina with some results for other crops obtained in other states. N.C. Agr. Expt. Sta., Agron. Inform. Circ. 104, 17pp., tables, charts, mimeogr. Raleigh. 1937. 275.29 N811Ag

Cooper, H.P., Hall, E.E., Rogers, W.B., Wallace, R.W., and Smith, R.L. Relative value of different brands of sodium nitrate in cotton production. S.C. Agr. Expt. Sta., Circ.56, 2pp., table. Clemson. [1937] 100 So8

"No significant differences were found in the yields of cotton from plots receiving equivalent amounts of ammonia from different brands of sodium nitrate."

Cotton methods for the largest profits in 1937. Prog. Farmer (Tex. ed.) 52(4):12,62, illus. April 1937. (Published at 1104 Insurance Bldg., Dallas, Tex.) 6 T311

Interview with D.T. Killough, agronomist of the Texas Agricultural Experiment Station.

Fiji. Department of agriculture. Annual bulletin of divisional reports, 1935. 62pp., tables. Suva, 1936. 25 F47Ba

Cotton industry division, annual report, 1935, by R. Lyon Field, pp.48-50. Singatoka experiment station--Annual report, by D.A. Donald, pp.50-59. Efforts to develop the production of Sea Island cotton are described.

Fomento del cultivo del algodon en Tucuman. Circulares de la estacion experimental agricola a los ingenios y a los caneros. Industria Azucarera 42(517):570-574. November 1936. (Published at Buenos Aires, Argentina) 65.8 In22

Encouragement of cotton cultivation in Tucuman. Circulars of the experiment station for agriculture, engineering and waterworks.

Gambia. Department of agriculture. The report...for the period ending 31st May, 1936. 14pp., tables. Bathurst, 1936. 24 G14

"Varieties of cotton were introduced from India in 1931. Of these Cambodia has been grown in small quantities and after five generations it is superior to the local Gambian variety, and is being multiplied up for distribution. The cotton crop generally was satisfactory."-Empire Cotton Growing Rev.,14(1):55. January 1937.

Gondim, Lopes. Como ter prejuizo e como ganhar dinheiro plantando algodao. Revista Algodoeira 2(15):7. December 1936. (Published at Recife, Brazil)   72.8 R32

How to lose and how to make money planting cotton.

Greene, H. Soil problems of the Anglo-Egyptian Sudan. Empire Jour. Expt. Agr. 5(17):1-10, illus. January 1937. (Published by Humphrey Milford, Oxford University Press, Amen House, Warwick Square, London, E.C.4, England) 10 Em7

The Sudan "contains three cotton-growing districts: the Gezira plain, of which part is irrigated from the Sennar dam, and the alluvial fans of the Gash and Baraka rivers, which permit flood-irrigation during their brief summer spate. Long-staple cotton is a recent introduction."

Hunnicutt, B.H. Lavoura de algodao. Revista da Sociedade Rural Brasileira. 17(197):20-21, illus. January 1937. (Published at Rua Libero Badaró N.45, Sao Paulo, Brazil)   9.2 B733

Cultivation of cotton.

Imperial bureau of soil science. Tropical soils in relation to tropical crops. Imperial Bur. Soil Sci., Tech. Commun. 34, 60pp., tables. Harpenden, England, 1936. 56.9 Im72

Cotton, pp.20-26. (References, pp.25-26)

Jio, K. The crop scientific study on the cotton cultivation in Taiwan. Formosan Agr. Rev. no.362, pp.16-45. January 1937. (Published at Taihoku, Formosa)   J22.5 F76

In Japanese.

Jio, Keisho. The crop scientific study on the cotton cultivation in Taiwan. Formosan Agr. Rev.no.363, pp.119-152. February 1937. (Published at Taihoku, Formosa)   J 22.5 F76

In Japanese.

Kime, P.H. Important factors in cotton growing in North Carolina. N.C. Agr. Expt. Sta., Agron. Inform. Circ. 106, 5pp., mimeogr. Raleigh. 1937.   275.29 N811Ag

Soil requirements, preparation of the land, time of planting, rate of planting, best varieties, distance between rows, distance between hills and number of plants per hill, cultivation, picking and storage, ginning, care and method of handling planting seed, are the factors described.

Kuykendall, R. Potash for cotton in the Delta foothills. Better Crops with Plant Food 21(4):9-10,41-42. February 1937. (Published by American Potash Institute, Inc., Investment Bldg., Washington, D.C.) 6 B46

Landeghem, A. Quinze années de culture du coton au Congo Belge, 1921-1936. Agriculture et Elevage au Congo Belge 11(3):38-39. March 1937. (Published at 34, rue de Stassart Bruxelles, Belgium) 26 Ag84
  Fifteen years of cotton cultivation in Belgian Congo, 1921-1936.

Legostaev, V.M. Distribution of cotton growing areas of Central Asia and southern Kazakstan according to water-supply. 111pp., illus., tables, charts. Tashkent, 1935. 72 L52
  At head of title: Sredneaziatskii nauchno-issledovatel'skii institut po khlopkovodstvu (Sredaznikhi)
  In Russian.

Marescalchi, A. La coltivazione del cotone all'asciutto nel Tavoliere di Puglia. Italia Vinicola ed Agraria 27(2):24-25. Jan. 20, 1937. (Published at Casalmonferrato, Italy) 95.8 Itl
  The cultivation of cotton in the dry regions of Tavolieri de Puglia.

Marques, Aloysio. O experimentalismo algodoeiro em Alagôas. Revista Algodoeira 2(15):8-10, illus. December 1936. (Published at Recife, Brazil) 72.8 R32
  Cotton experiments in Alagôas.

Miles, G.F. A new definition of "quality" for cottonseed. Amer. Ginner and Cotton Oil Miller. 14(6):4-6, illus. February 1937. (Published at P.O. Box 504, Little Rock, Ark.) 72.8 Am35
  "To the other specifications for high

quality seed such as trueness to type, freedom from mixtures and weeds; and viability of the seed, they have added one more feature, namely, freedom of the seed from surface seed-borne disease organisms."

El nuevo método para la desinfección de la semilla de algodón. El esterilizador a vapor vivo Rylander para desmotadoras y fábricas de aceite. Gaceta Algodonera 12(156):17,19, illus. Jan.31,1937. (Published at Reconquista 331, Casilla Correo 550, Buenos Aires, Argentina) 72.8 G11

A new method for disinfecting cotton seed. Rylander live steam sterilizer for gins and oil factories.

Piscugin, I.N. [New varieties of cotton for the Fargana valley.] Bor'ba za Khlopok no.8-9, pp.119-122. August/September 1935. (Published at Tashkent, U.S.S.R.) 72.8 B64
In Russian.
"Kolknoznik, No.5F, Pima F. and Kim No. 2017 are the most suitable strains."-Empire Cotton Growing Rev. 13(3):245. July 1936.

Sasaki, Takashi. Considerations of cotton culture in South Manchu. Crop Sci. Soc., Japan, Proc. 8(4):516-526. December 1936. (Published at Tokyo, Japan) J 22.5 C88
In Japanese.

Se han introducido al país nuevas variedades de semilla de algodon. Revista de la Sociedad Rural de Rosario 16(178):38. December 1936. (Published at Boulevard Orono 2498, Rosario, Argentina) 9 Sc14

New varieties of cottonseed have been introduced in the country.

Supply of cotton seed short. Acco Press 15(3): 5. March 1937. (Published by Anderson, Clayton & Co., Houston, Tex.) 6 Ac2

"A letter from Mr. W.L. Clayton addressed to the Fort Worth Star-Telegram together with that publication's pertinent comments concerning its contents," are given. Need for healthy planting seed in drought-stricken areas is pointed out.

Texas Agricultural experiment station. Report of cotton variety test at the Blackland experiment station, by H.E. Rea. 14pp., tables. College Station. 1936   72 T31

La vernalisation du cotôn. Assoc. Coton. Colon. Bull. Trimestriel 35(25):26-27. Jan.1,1937. (Published at 55, Rue de Châteaudun, Paris XIXe, France)   72.9 As7
, Vernalization of cotton.
From Revue de Botanique Appliquèe et d'Agriculture Tropicale, November 1936.

Wells, W.G. Thinning and spacing of cotton. Queensland Agr. Jour. 47(2):219-220. Feb.1, 1937. (Published by Department of Agriculture and Stock, Brisbane, Queensland, Australia)   23 Q33

Wille, Johannes E., Carrera, José Lamas, and Tijero B. El cultivo del algodón en los valles de los departmentos de Lambayeque y Libertad. La Vida Agricola 14(159):151-155. February 1937. (Published at Lima, Peru) 9.8 V66
The cultivation of cotton in the valleys of the Departments of Lambayeque and Libertad.

Wolf, George. Cotton seed treatment. Amer. Cotton Grower 2(10):21. March 1937. (Published at 535 Gravier St., New Orleans, La.) 72.8 Am32

Diseases

Bailey, E.H. Prevent cotton rust by using potash. Miss. Co-op. News 8(8):3. February 1937. (Published at 236 1/2 Capitol St., Jackson, Miss.)   72.8 M69

Cotton tests. Mid-So. Cotton News 14(8):2. March 1937. (Published at 822 Falls Bldg., Memphis, Tenn.)   72.8 C8295
"Reports of studies on the Control of Cotton Wilt and 'Rust' or Potash Hunger, Conducted by the University of Arkansas College of Agriculture, Cotton Branch Experiment Station, Lee County, Marianna, Arkansas."

Fawcett, G.L. Notas sobre algunas enfermedades del algodonero. Tucuman, Estacion Experimental Agricola, Circ. 52, 8pp., illus. Tucuman. 1936. 102.5 T79
Notes on some diseases of the cotton plant.
Extracts in Gaceta Algodonero 12(156): 7-9. Jan.31,1937; La Chacra 7(77):95-96. March 1937.

King, C.J. A method for the control of cotton root rot in the irrigated southwest. U.S. Dept. Agr., Bur. Plant Indus. Circ. 425, 9pp., illus., charts. Washington, 1937. 1 Ag84C

Odriozola, Manuel E. Lo que significa para el Perú, la emfermedad debida a un hongo, llamada vulgarmente wilt, que ataca al algodonero. Boletin de la Compania Administradora del Guano 11(8):383-394. August 1935. (Published at Zarate 455, Lima, Peru) 57.9 C73B
The significance of the fungus disease cotton wilt for Peru.
"This is a general discussion of the disease and factors influencing its depredations in Peru, including the question of resistant varieties."-Expt. Sta. Rec. 76(2):201. February 1937.

Peltier, George L. Distribution and prevalence of ozonium root rot in the shelterbelt zone of Texas. Phytopathology 27(2): 145-158, illus., table, chart. February 1937. (Published at Cor. Lime and Green Sts., Lancaster, Pa.) 464.8 P56

Insects

Boll weevil control plans are explained. Control on cotton plants with hairy stems and leaves more effective. Tex. Co-op. News 17(3):5 Mar.15,1937. (Published by Texas Co-operative Publishing Co., Inc., 601 Taylor St., Fort Worth, Tex.) 72.9 T315F
Experiments at the Texas Agricultural Experiment Station are noted.

Costa Lima, A. da. Um novo Eumolpideo inimigo do algodoeiro (Coleoptera: Chrysomeloidea). O Campo [Brazil] 7(83):35-36, illus. November 1936. (Published at Rio de Janeiro, Brazil) 9.2 C15
   A new Eumolpina enemy of cotton (Coleoptera: Chrysomela)

Franceschi, A.V. Una grave amenaza al cultivo de algodon. Revista de Agricultura de Puerto Rico 28(2):280-283, illus. December 1936. (Published by Departmento de Agricultura y Trabajo, San Juan, Puerto Rico) 8 R325
   A grave menace to cotton cultivation (the pink bollworm).

Jackson, A.D. How to poison boll weevil. Acco Press 15(3):12. March 1937. (Published by Anderson, Clayton & Co., Houston, Tex.) 6 Ac2

Kamal, M. Recent advances in the control of the pink boll-worm (Platyedra gossypiella, Saunders) by natural enemies. Société Royale Entomologique d'Egypte, Bulletin 20:259-271, illus., charts. 1936. (Published at Cairo, Egypt) 420 Eg9

A lagarta rosada nos algodoaes de Sao Paulo. Sociedade Rural Brasileira, Revista 17(198): 36-37. February 1937. (Published at Rua Libero Badaro, 314, Sao Paulo, Brazil) 9.2 B733
   Pink bollworm of cotton.

Lebnan, B. La lutte contre le ver de la feuille du coton. L'Union des Agriculteurs d'Egypte, Bull.35(279):12-17. January 1937. (Published at 25, Rue Cheikh Abou El-Sebaa, Cairo, Egypt) 24 Un32
   The struggle against the cotton leaf worm.

MacGill, Elsie I. The biology of thysanoptera with reference to the cotton plant. VIII. The relation between variations in temperature and the life cycle. Ann. Appl. Biol. 24(1): 95-109, tables, charts. February 1937. (Published by Cambridge University Press,

Fetter Lane, E.C.4, London, England) 442.8 An72

References, p.109.

The study of the effect of sudden, non-permanent variations in temperature on the life-cycle of the insect, Thrips tabaci, is described.

Rekach, V.N., and Dobretsova, T.A. Survey of insects injurious to utility and forage crops in Transcaucasia. Gandja. Zakavkazskii Nauchno-issledovatel'skii Khlopkovyi Institut. Trudy (Transcaucasia Cotton Research Institute. Trans.) 45, 236pp., illus., tables, charts. Tiflis. 1935. 72.9 G15

In Russian. Summary in English.

"Insects injuring cotton amount to 156 species, foremost among them being the orders Coleoptera and Lepidoptera, comprising 47 and 43 species respectively."

Sea-Island cotton revival seen as definite possibility. Com. Fertilizer 54(4):32-34, illus., chart. April 1937. (Published by Walter W. Brown Publishing Co., 223 Courtland St., N.E., Atlanta, Ga.) 57.8 C73

Boll weevil control is the main factor necessary for revival of sea island cotton. A.W.P.A. project makes this a possibility.

Velho, Regis. Insectos que atacam os algodoeiros. Revista Algodoeira 2(16):5-6. January 1937. (Published at Recife, Brazil) 72.8 R32

Insects which attack cotton.

[Welch, J.H.] The low down on the cotton fleahopper. Tex. Farming and Citricult. 13(9):7-8, illus., table. March 1937. (Published by E.C. Watson Publishing Co., Harlingen, Tex.) 80 T31

Efforts of the Texas Agricultural Extension Service, cooperating with the U.S. Bureau of Entomology, to control the cotton fleahopper are described.

Wille, Johannes E., Carrera, Jose Lamas, and Tijero B., Luis. El arrebiatado y otros insectos daninos al algodonero en los Valles del Norte del Perú. Lima, Estacion Experimental Agricola de la Molina, Boletín no.9, 85pp., illus, charts. Lima, Peru. 1936. 102.5 L622B

The cotton stainer and other insects injurious to cotton in the Valley of the North of Peru.

Farm Engineering

Argentine Republic. Junta nacional del algodón. Como debe cosecharse el algodón. Argentine Rep. Junta Nacional del Algodon [Pub.] 17, 2pp., illus. Buenos Aires. 1937. 281.3729 Ar3

How to harvest cotton.

Bealle, James S. Dixie needs no cotton picker. Forum and Cent. 97(4):224-229. April 1937. (Published at 570 Lexington Ave., New York, N.Y.)

"The Southern farmer has no great need for a cotton picking machine. He can arrange for his cotton to be picked for less money under the present system."

Harvester engineer works thirty years on cotton picker. East. Dealer in Impl. & Vehicles 31(2):26,28, illus. Mar.11,1937. (Published at 533 Drexel Bldg., Philadelphia, Pa.) 58.8 Ea7

Harvester cotton picker invented by T.A. Johnston is described.

Also in Farm Mach. and Equipment (1839): 7-8,42. Mar.15,1937.

I.H.C. Cotton picker. Still experimental after 30 years of trying, but success is in sight. Ariz. Producer 15(25):7,33. Mar.15,1937. (Published at 313 North Third Ave., Phoenix, Ariz.)

Describes the International Harvester Company cotton picker invented by E.A. Johnson.

International harvester cotton picker. Mfrs. Rec. 106(3):52, illus. March 1937. (Published at Commerce and Water Sts., Baltimore, Md.) 297.8 M31

"The International Harvester Company of

America Inc." thinks "the time is still remote when cotton pickers will be placed generally on the market."

Mechanical cotton picker. Mangt. Rev. 25(11): 342-343. November 1936. (Published by American Management Association, 330 West 42d St., New York, N.Y.) 280.8 M312
    Editorial from the New York Times, September 3, 1936.

Medvedev, I.D. The economical analyse of machinery for the cotton pests in the Uzbekian SSR. Lenin Acad. Agr. Sci. Inst. Plant Protection, Bull. Plant Protection (Ser. 3), no.8, pp.153-166, tables. 1936. (Published at Leningrad, U.S.S.R.) 423.92 L54C
    In Russian.

Meisakhovich, Ia. A. Mechanization of the cotton seed disinfection with sulphuric acid. Lenin Acad. Agr. Sci., Inst. Plant Protection, Bull. Plant Protection (Ser.3) no.8, pp.89-96, tables. 1936. (Published at Leningrad, U.S.S.R.) 423.92 L54C
    In Russian.

Meisakhovich, Ia. A., and Medvedev, I.D. Mechanization of cotton seed disinfection with formaldehyde. Lenin Acad. Agr. Sci., Inst. Plant Protection, Bull. Plant Protection (Ser.3), no.8, pp.77-88, illus., tables. 1936. (Published at Leningrad, U.S.S.R.) 423.92 L54C
    In Russian.

Speculating on mechanical cotton pickers. Barron's 16(40):20. Oct.5,1936. (Published at 30 Kilby St., Boston, Mass.) 284.8 B27
    The five principles upon which manufacturers are working are listed. "Experience has been that ...unless the product is taken away from the research departments and put into circulation, the day of its perfection will be definitely delayed."

Una invención que quiza revolucione la industria algodonera. La Hacienda 31(11):377, illus. November 1936. (Published at 20 Vesey St., New York, N.Y.) 6 H11

An invention that will revolutionize the cotton industry.

The Rust cotton picker is described.

Farm Management

Biggest cotton plantation in the U.S. is the sixty square miles of Delta & Pine Land Co. of Scott, Mississippi. Its ownership is English, its management Mississippian, its labor 1,000 negro sharecropper families, and its 1936 net $153,600. A fortunate freak in cotton. Fortune 15(3):125-132,156,158,160, illus., chart. March 1937. (Published by Time Inc., 160 Maple St., Jersey City, N.J.)

El costo de produccion del algodon. Boletin Mensual no.22,pp.1-5, tables, charts, mimeogr. February 1937. (Published by Ministerio de Agricultura, Junta Nacional del Algodon, Buenos Aires, Argentina.)

The cost of production of cotton.

Farm Social Problems

American civil liberties union. The struggle for civil liberty on the land; the story of the recent struggles of land-owning farmers, of share-croppers, tenants and farm laborers for the right to organize, strike and picket. 47pp. New York, [1937] 283 Am36

Descriptions of the strike of cotton pickers in the San Joaquin Valley and of the attempts of sharecroppers in Alabama and Arkansas to organize are included.

Arkansas State policy committee. Agricultural labor problems in Arkansas. Sub-committee report. Ark. State Policy Com., Pub. Paper 1, 34pp., tables, charts. [Little Rock] 1936. 280.9 Ar43

Includes problems of sharecroppers on cotton plantations.

141

Institute on Southern regional development and
the social sciences. Review and summary of
findings, Institute on Southern regional
development and the social sciences, June
17-27,1936, Chapel Hill, University of North
Carolina. 34pp., mimeogr, [n.p., 1936]
280.9 In793

Cooperation in Production

Barre, C.B. Marketing progress of one-variety
cotton in Oklahoma and other states. Okla.
Agr. Expt. Sta. Current Farm Econ. Ser.49,
10(1):17-20, table. February 1937. (Published by the Department of Agricultural
Economics, Oklahoma A. & M. College, Stillwater, Okla.) 100 Ok4
    The quality of cotton produced in onevariety communities is noted. The following
methods of improving its marketing are suggested: Better ginning; Classification for
the farmer; Market news service; Advertising
the product.

Bassi, Edoardo. Cotone e cooperazione.
Cooperazione Rurale 6(2):18-20, illus.
Feb.15,1937. (Published by Federazione
Italiana Consorzi Agrari, Via 24, Maggio
43, Rome, Italy) 280.28 C7835
    Cotton and cooperation.

Dhonan, L.A. Profits in improved cotton varieties. Boys have a cotton and pig club. Ark.
Farmer 29(14):4. Mar.15,1937. (Published
by Stanley Andrews Publishing Co., Little
Rock, Ark.)
    One variety cotton community is recommended.

East Texas chamber sponsors single variety
communities. Cotton Ginners' Jour. 8(6):
6,17. March 1937. (Published by Texas
Cotton Ginners' Association, Inc., 109 North
Second Ave., Dallas, Tex.) 304.8 C824
    Rules and regulations for the "$1,000,
five-year, one-variety-cotton community contest being sponsored by the East Texas Chamber of Commerce" are given.
    Also in Farm and Ranch 56(5):7. Mar.1,1937.

Looking ahead. Cotton Digest 9(24):5-6.
Mar.20,1937. (Published at 710 Cotton
Exchange Bldg., Houston, Tex.) 286.82
C822
   An editorial urging cooperation to
improve cotton production.

Ousley, Clarence. Good planting seed. Cotton
and Cotton Oil Press 38(9):14. Feb.27,1937.
(Published at 3116-18 Commerce St., Dallas,
Tex.) 304.8 C822
   The advantages of one-variety communities
are discussed.
   Also in Acco Press 15(3):6-7. March 1937.

Single variety pays dividends. Coupland
community project. Cotton Ginners' Jour.
8(7):37-38. April 1937. (Published by
Texas Cotton Ginners' Association, Inc.,
109 North Second Ave., Dallas, Tex.)
304.8 C824

Staples, Robert T. Advantages of one-variety
cotton from a spinner's viewpoint. Cotton
Ginners' Jour. 8(7):20,43. April 1937.
(Published by Texas Cotton Ginners' Asso-
ciation, Inc., 109 North Second Ave., Dallas,
Tex.) 304.8 C824.

PREPARATION

General

Bennett, Charles A. Steam heaters for cotton conditioners. Cotton Ginners' Jour.
8(7):9-10,40, illus., table. April 1937.
(Published by Texas Cotton Ginners' Association, Inc., 109 North Second Ave., Dallas, Tex.) 304.8 C824
   Construction of such heaters is described.

Ginning

Adams, Orville. Maintenance of the electrical
equipment in the gin. Overhauling and repair
work on motors very necessary for efficiency.
Cotton and Cotton Oil Press 38(9):3-4. Feb.
27,1937. (Published at 3116-18 Commerce St.,
Dallas, Tex.) 304.8 C822

Bennett, Charles A., and Gerdes, F.L. Improving cotton gins for better service. Cotton Ginners' Jour. 8(6):5,10-12. March 1937. (Published by Texas Cotton Ginners' Association, Inc., 109 North Second Ave., Dallas, Tex.) 304.8 C824

Lichte, F.E. Ginning wet cotton. Cotton Ginners' Jour. 8(7):11. April 1937. (Published by Texas Cotton Ginners' Association, Inc., 109 North Second Ave., Dallas, Tex.) 304.8 C824

Rylander cotton drier and cleaner creating much interest. Cotton Ginners' Jour. 8(6):14. March 1937. (Published by Texas Cotton Ginners' Association, Inc., 109 North Second Ave., Dallas, Tex.) 304.8 C824

Baling

Basombrío, E. Ensayos sobre el abonamiente del algodón en la hacienda Humaya. Boletin Compania Administradora del Guano 12(12):451-456. December 1936. (Published at Lima, Peru) 57.9 C73B
    Experiments on the baling of cotton on the Humaya farm.

MARKETING

General

Cobb, C.A. 1937 no year for a big cotton crop. Prog. Farmer (Car.-Va. ed.) 52(4):14, chart. April 1937. (Published at Raleigh, N.C.) 6 P945
    Outlook for 1937 is given.

Cotton's record year of output and consumption. "Outside" growths again in van of rise. Textile Mercury and Argus 47th Ann. Trade Rev. Sup., pp.22,31, table. Feb.19,1937. (Published at 41, Spring Gardens, Manchester, England) 304.8 T318
    Annual review of 1936 cotton trade.

Cox, A.B. Cotton and customers. If South cannot find markets it will be forced to compete with other sections. Cotton Digest 9(22):

6,15. Mar.6,1937. (Published at 710 Cotton Exchange Bldg., Houston, Tex.) 286.82 C822

"If the South cannot find markets for cotton it will be forced into food production and manufacturing."

Davidson, Robert. Cotton, its uses and abuses. Pacific Rural Press 133(1):20. Jan.2,1937. (Published at 560 Howard St., San Francisco, Calif.) 6 P112

Uses of cotton are mentioned and the marketing of California irrigated cotton is commented upon.

Miller, Dale. Cotton markets must be restored. Tex. Weekly 13(12):4-5. Mar.20,1937. (Published at Dallas Athletic Club Bldg., Dallas, Tex.) 280.8 T31

Current discussion of the measures necessary to solve the South's economic problems is commented upon.

Molyneaux, Peter. The cotton south and American trade policy. 63pp., tables. New York, National peace conference, 1936. (World affairs books, no.17) 280.8 W89

The author describes the effect of the World War on the South as well as the effect of the American foreign trade policy on the production and marketing of cotton.

Parker, Walter. To promote lasting prosperity, lower tariffs and free investment capital. Cotton and Cotton Oil Press 38(9):16. Feb. 27,1937. (Published at 3116-18 Commerce St., Dallas, Tex.) 304.8 C822

"The South needs its raw-cotton industry, but cannot hope to hold it unless the United States obeys the rules applicable to a surplus-producing world creditor status; clear world trade channels; put an end to tax-subsidized government competition with tax-paying business, and rely upon efficient, low-cost production to meet world competition.

The South's stake in trade. Amer. Cotton Grower 2(10):5. March 1937. (Published at 535 Gravier St., New Orleans, La.) 72.8 Am32

The author lists "some evident considerations that must be in any cotton plan."

Statistical position of cotton improves, but foreigners turn to other growths. Annalist 49(1253):135, table. Jan.22,1937. (Published by New York Times Co., Times Square, New York, N.Y.) 284.8 N48
Review of 1936.

United States Federal trade commission. Federal trade commission reports on agricultural income investigation. 25pp., mimeogr. [Washington, D.C.] 1937.
Cotton markets, pp.6-7; Recommendations with special reference to the cotton trade, pp.19-21.
The commission recommends study of Southern delivery, of methods of determining spot quotations, and of payment to farmers on grade and staple.
Extracts in Domestic Commerce 19(7):144-145. Mar.10,1937; Domestic Commerce 19(8): 156-170, tables, charts. Mar.20,1937.

Competition

American cotton manufacturer's association. Proceedings of the fortieth annual convention...Pinehurst, North Carolina, May 1-2, 1936. 170pp. [Charlotte, N.C.] 1936. 304.9 Am3.

Applegate, La Rue. Textile consumption four billion pounds: Profit margins more substantial. Annalist 49(1253):127, tables, charts. Jan.22,1937. (Published by New York Times Co., Times Square, New York, N.Y.) 284.8 N48
This review of the year 1936 and outlook for 1937 compares the cotton, wool, silk and rayon industries.

Argentine trade outlook improving. Textile business prospects. Manchester Guardian Com. 34(868):118. Feb.5,1937. .(Published at Guardian Bldg., 3 Cross St., Manchester, 2, England) 286.8 M315

[Bombay millowners association] Progress of cotton spinning and weaving mills in India, annual statement. Indian Textile Jour. 47(556):131. January 1937. (Published at

Military Square, Fort, Bombay, India) 304.8 In2

British textiles exhibition. Indian cotton committee entertains Sir Ramaswamy Mudaliar. Joint committee's comprehensive display. Manchester Chamber of Com. Mo. Rec. 48(2): 73-75. Feb.28,1937. (Published at Ship Canal House, King St., Manchester, 2, England) 287 M31

Some uses of cotton are noted. The increased use of Indian cotton and the Ottawa Agreement are mentioned.

The broader significance of the Japanese quota arrangement. Cotton [Atlanta] 101(3):67. March 1937. (Published by W.R.C. Smith Publishing Company, Grant Bldg., Atlanta, Ga.) 304.8 C823

Editorial.

Buhlmann, A.V. Are we making progress in the textile industry? Amer. Dyestuff Reptr. 26(4):P99-P101. Feb.22,1937. (Published by Howes Publishing Co., Inc., 440 Fourth Ave., New York, N.Y.) 306.3 An3

Address at annual meeting of American Association of Textile Chemists and Colorists, Providence, R.I., December 5, 1936.

The author concludes that "the rehabilitation of the textile industry, is on the way."

C. I. O. tackles textiles. Textile World 87(4):701. March 1937. (Published by McGraw-Hill Publishing Co., Inc., 330 West 42d St., New York, N.Y.) 304.8 T315

Plans of the Committee for Industrial Organization are noted.

Carlisle, Prince M. Increased production endangers present strong market position. Textile Bull. 51(25):3,31. Feb.18,1937. (Published by Clark Publishing Co., 118 West Fourth St., Charlotte, N.C.) 304.8 So82

The present situation in the print cloth market is described.

Carlisle, Prince M. Textile merchandising methods have been modernized. Textile Bull. 51(24):12,68. Feb.11,1937. (Published by Clark Publishing Co., 118 West Fourth St., Charlotte, N.C.) 304.8 So82

Clark, David. Annual machinery increase figures for the South. Textile Bull. 51(24):34-38, 50,53, tables. Feb.11,1937. (Published by Clark Publishing Co., 118 West Fourth St., Charlotte, N.C.) 304.8 So82
"Tabulations give the name and location of each mill in the South that installed additional spindles during 1936, together with the totals by States."

Clucas, W.E. Lancashire looks to the government. Textile Mercury and Argus 47th Ann. Trade Rev. Sup., pp.11-12. Feb.19,1937. (Published at 41, Spring Gardens, Manchester, England) 304.8 T318
Outlook for the Lancashire cotton-Textile industry for 1937.

Commercial agreement between Japan and Australia. Mitsubishi Mo. Circ. no.160, p.24. February 1937. (Published by Mitsubishi Economic Research Bureau, Marunouchi 3, Tokyo, Japan) 280.8 M69
Quotas of Japanese cotton and rayon piece goods and of Australian wool goods are given.

Conditions in Japan. Japan shows more all-round industrial development, the cotton and rayon trades having got themselves into troubles, calling for reorganization, the pace of expansion is slackening. Textile Manfr. 62(744):453-454, tables. December 1936. (Published by Emmott & Co., Ltd., 31 King St., West, Manchester, 3, England) 304.8 T3126

[Cotton-textile institute] Intensive program for the promotion of cotton goods. Cotton Trade Jour. 17(12):2. Mar.20,1937. (Published at 810 Union St., New Orleans, La.) 72.8 C8214
Plans approved at "the organization meeting of a Joint Cotton Promotional Advisory Com-

mittee of cotton spinners and raw cotton shippers in the Institute's Washington office."

The cotton trade in 1936. Year of consolidation for Lancashire industry; but India trade setback holds up recovery. Textile Mercury and Argus 47th Ann. Trade Rev. Sup., pp.16-17. Feb.19,1937. (Published at 41, Spring Gardens, Manchester, England) 304.8 T318

Crawford, M.D.C. Strikes are a waste, mill men should run plants, Hillman says. Daily News Rec. no.64, pp.1,13. Mar.18,1937. (Published at 8 East 13th St., New York, N.Y.) 286.8 N48
An interview with Sidney Hillman, leader in the textile union movement.

Dr. Murchison given reception. Fibre and Fabric 90(2718):6-7. Mar.6,1937. (Published by Wade Publishing Co., 465 Main St., Kendall Square, Cambridge, Mass.) 304.8 F44
An account by Dr. Claudius T. Murchison of the trade mission to Japan is given in part.

Export of cotton tissues. Mitsubishi Mo. Circ. no.160, p.24, table. February 1937. (Published by Mitsubishi Economic Research Bureau, Marunouchi 3, Tokyo, Japan) 280.8 M69
"According to statistics compiled by the Japan Federation of Cotton Tissues Manufacturers' Associations, exports of cotton tissues from Japan during the year 1936 totaled 2,707,799,000 sq. yds." The table shows a comparison of exports from Japan and from Great Britain by country of destination.

Good times are here again! Declared cotton manufacturers, who saw real profits in 1936. Textile World 87(3):141, charts. Feb.28,1937. (Published by McGraw-Hill Publishing Co., Inc., 330 West 42d St., New York, N.Y.) 304.8 T315
The cotton-textile industry in the United States for 1936 is reviewed.

Graves, John Temple, II. The textile mission
to Japan. Textile Bull. 51(25):8-9. Feb.18,
1937. (Published by Clark Publishing Co.,
118 West Fourth St., Charlotte, N.C.)
304.8 So82
   The author comments on Mr. Donald Comer's
suggestion for "triangular trade" between
Japan, the United States and other countries.

Greenbie, Sydney. Cotton, cotton everywhere.
Christian Sci. Monitor, Weekly Mag. Sec.
pp.1-2, illus. Feb.10,1937. (Published
by Christian Science Publishing Co., 1
Norway St., Boston, Mass.)
   The problems facing the world textile
conference in Washington in April, 1937,
are mentioned.

Hillman, Sidney. Poor organization causes
industrial strife. Daily News Rec. no.66,
pp.1,8. Mar.20,1937. (Published at 8 East
13th St., New York, N.Y.) 286.8 N48
   "Statement of Sidney Hillman, chairman
of the Textile Workers' Organizing Committee,
on the purposes and policies approved by the
first meeting of the T.W.O.C."

International committee. Cotton Digest 9(25):
9,12-13. Mar.27,1937. (Published at 710
Cotton Exchange Bldg., Houston, Tex.)
286.82 C822
   The American members of the International
Textile Committee are announced. Japanese
members have not yet been appointed.

Japan threatens U.S. with her cotton goods but
domestic industry helps itself. Textile
World 87(3):118-119, tables. Feb.28,1937.
(Published by McGraw-Hill Publishing Co.,
Inc., 330 West 42d St., New York, N.Y.)
304.8 T315

Lee, Herbert W. Factors in the brighter outlook for cotton. Spinners are putting their
house in order. Textile Mercury and Argus
47th Ann. Trade Rev. Sup., p.15. Feb.19,
1937. (Published at 41, Spring Gardens,
Manchester, England) 304.8 T318

McAllister, H.S. Textile securities in the
   South.   South. Banker 68(1):19,36-38,
   chart. January 1937. (Published at 900
   Walton Bldg., Atlanta, Ga.) 284.8 So8
      "The gradual movement of spindles from
   the North to the South during the past
   decade has made the textile industry the
   principal industry of the South, insofar as
   the amount of money invested in these plants
   is concerned."

[Manchester chamber of commerce] Annual
   meeting of members. Need for restoration
   of staple export trades. Mr. W.E. Clucas's
   fourth presidential address. Manchester
   Chamber of Com. Mo. Rec. 48(2):55-63. Feb.
   28,1937. (Published at Ship Canal House,
   King St., Manchester, 2, England) 287 M31
      The address includes a statement on the
   cotton trade position.

Murchison, Claudius T. An account of the tex-
   tile mission's visit to Japan. Textile Bull.
   52(1):3-5. Mar.4,1937. (Published by Clark
   Publishing Co., 118 West Fourth St., Charlotte,
   N.C.) 304.8 So82
      "An address at a dinner of the Textile
   Square Club at the McAlpine Hotel, New York
   City, Thursday evening February 25,1937."
      Extracts in Textile World 87(4):701. March
   1937.

Nieh, Kanyo. Cotton industry in China. Phenome-
   nal growth of manufacture progress towards
   self-sufficiency in production of raw material.
   Inspection and Com. Jour. 7(12):12. December
   1936. (Published at 1040 N. Soochow Road,
   Shanghai, China) 286.8 Ex67
      Extracts from an address to the Young Men's
   Club, Shanghai.

Orvis, Homer W. Japan cotton situation. Serious
   threat of Orient textile imports into U.S. has
   been peaceably settled. Cotton Digest 9(22):
   10. Mar.6,1937. (Published at 710 Cotton
   Exchange Bldg., Houston, Tex.) 286.82 C822

Overseas trade in cotton textiles. The year's
   story in figures. Textile Mercury and Argus
   47th Ann. Trade Rev. Sup., pp.25, 27, tables.
   Feb.19,1937. (Published at 41, Spring Gardens,

Manchester, England) 304.8 T318
   Lancashire exports.

Partington, Harold. Cotton trade revival.
   The effects of monetary policy. Textile
   Weekly 19(470):305,307. Mar.5,1937.
   (Published at 49, Deansgate, Manchester,
   3, England)   304.8 T3127
      "In a lecture to the Preston and District
   Textile Managers' Association, February 5,
   1937."

Philip, Robert W. The story of the Japanese
   textile quota arrangement. Cotton [Atlanta]
   101(3):68-73, illus. March 1937. (Published by W.R.C. Smith Publishing Company,
   Grant Bldg., Atlanta, Ga.) 304.8 C823
      A report by the secretary of the American
   Textile Mission to Japan.

Protocol to the convention regarding the commercial relations between India and Japan.
   Shipments of raw cotton from India to Japan
   and of cotton piece-goods from Japan to
   India. Indian Trade Jour. 123(1590):1289,
   tables. Dec.10,1936. (Published by the
   Department of Commercial Intelligence and
   Statistics, 1, Council House St., Calcutta,
   India)   286.8 In24
      Shipments of raw cotton for the year end-
   ing December 31, 1935, and of cloth for the
   year ending March 31, 1936, are given.

Rayon and staple fibre. This year will be
   industry's great testing time. Dangers
   of sacrificing quality for cheapness. Textile Mercury and Argus 47th Ann. Trade Rev.
   Sup., p.55, tables. Feb.19,1937. (Published at 41, Spring Gardens, Manchester,
   England)   304.8 T318
      Outlook for 1937.

Roy, V. The present position of jute in Bengal.
   Indian Jour. Econ. 16(2):115-120. October
   1935. (Issued by the Dept. of Economics and
   Commerce, University of Allahabad, Allahabad,
   India)   280.8 In22
      The lack of an effective market and a con-
   tinued over-supply of the crop has brought
   the price of jute down to a "ridiculous

level." As a means of raising the price the compulsory restriction of the total area of cultivation has been demanded by a considerable section of the public. The Development Commissioner, however, advocated the scheme of voluntary restriction. The press and the public are not enthusiastic about the plan. The proposal of the Press for "legalizing the minimum price of raw jute" is not thought to be feasible.

Silveira, Osman. O que era em 1928, e o que é actualmente a industria algodoeira em Pernambuco. Revista Algodoeira 2(16):12-14, illus., tables. January 1937. (Published at Recife, Brazil) 72.8 R32

The cotton [textile] industry of Pernambuco of 1928 and now.

[Southern commissioners of agriculture] Commissioners of agriculture urge foreign market expansion. Cotton Trade Jour.17(9):1. Feb. 27,1937. (Published at 810 Union St., New Orleans, La.) 72.8 C8214

Resolutions adopted at the last meeting are given.

Text of textile agreement of the U.S. Japanese industries. Cotton Trade Jour. 17(9):1,4. Feb.27,1937. (Published at 810 Union St., New Orleans, La.) 72.8 C8214

"Under the recently negotiated quota agreement limiting shipments of Japanese cotton piece goods to the United States for the next two years...[a] committee of ten members, including three American and two Japanese members in the United States and two American and three Japanese members in Japan, is to be organized and begin functioning on or before April 1."

Also in Fibre and Fabric 90(2717):12. Feb.27,1937.

Textile boom pushes mill activity over 1929 rate and resurrects an antique: profits. Textile World 87(3):112-113, charts. Feb. 28, 1937. (Published by McGraw-Hill Publishing Co., Inc., 330 West 42d St., New York, N.Y.) 304.8 T315

Annual review of the textile industry in the United States for 1936.

Textile institute to promote campaign. Cotton
Digest 9(21):11-12. Feb.27,1937. (Published
at 710 Cotton Exchange Bldg., Houston, Tex.)
286.82 C822
"Plans for a broadened, intensive cotton
goods promotional program under the direction
of the Cotton-Textile Institute were approved
this week at the organization meeting of a
joint cotton promotional advisory committee
of cotton spinners and raw cotton shippers
in the Institute's Washington office."

Textile securities move with the trend and so
stockholders get a break. Textile World
87(3):120, tables, chart. Feb.28,1937.
(Published by McGraw-Hill Publishing Co.,
Inc., 330 West 42d St., New York, N.Y.)
304.8 T315
The market for 1936 is reviewed.

Textile workers' organizing committee. Research department. Table breakdown of
textile industry into components. Daily
News Rec. no.74,p.16, table. Mar.30,1937.
(Published at 8 East 13th St., New York,
N.Y.) 286.8 N48
Table shows geography, the number of
operatives employed, number of mills, their
location and other pertinent information.

United States Tariff commission. Comparative
statistics of imports into the United States
for consumption, by countries for the calendar years 1931-1935 inclusive...Vol.V, Group
3.-Textiles. Part 1.-Cotton and other vegetable fibers (except countable cotton cloth),
straw or other fiber hats and materials, miscellaneous textile products. W.P.A. Statis.
Proj. 65-31-2075, 437pp. tables, chart, processed. Richmond. 1936. 173 T17Cst

The Washington conference. Textile Weekly
19(472):363,364. Mar.19,1937. (Published
at 49, Deansgate, Manchester, 3, England)
304.8 T3127
Editorial on the Tripartite Textile Technical Conference to be held in Washington,
April 2, 1937.

Wiggins, W.M. Defects in current management must be remedied. Britain's chance to lead world trade revival. Textile Mercury and Argus 47th Ann. Trade Rev. Sup., pp.13-14, Feb.19,1937. (Published at 41, Spring Gardens, Manchester, England) 304.8 T318
   Outlook for the Lancashire cotton spinning industry for 1937.

Woolf, Douglas G. Precision, the next step to profits in textiles. Textile World 87(3): 121. Feb.28,1937. (Published by McGraw-Hill Publishing Co., Inc., 330 West 42d St., New York, N.Y.) 304.8 T315

The world textile industry. The forthcoming technical tripartite conference at Washington. Textile Weekly 19(472):367. Mar.19,1937. (Published at 49, Deansgate, Manchester, 3, England) 304.8 T3127

Supply and Movement

Argentine Republic. Ministerio de agricultura. Junta nacional del algodon. Censo algodonero de la Republica Argentina, ano 1935-36. Argentine Rep. Junta nacional del algodon, [Pub.] 16, 312pp., tables, charts. Buenos Aires. 1936. 281.3729 Ar3
   Cotton census of the Argentine Republic, 1935-36.

Attention to quality. Cotton Digest 9(25) 4. Mar.27,1937. (Published at 710 Cotton Exchange Bldg., Houston, Tex.) 286.82 C822
   Editorial commending the work of the Texas Cotton Association and the East Texas Chamber of Commerce toward improving the quality of Texas cotton.

Chang, C.C. An estimate of China's farms and crops. 21pp., tables, charts. [Nanking, 1932] 281.184 C36
   Tables V and VI and map XII show distribution of cotton acreage and production by provinces and regions.

Le conditionnement des cotons soudanais, et le role de l'Association cotonnière coloniale. Association Cotonnière Coloniale Bulletin

Trimestriel 35 (25):9-10. Jan.1,1937.
(Published at 55, Rue de Chateaudun, Paris XIXe, France) .72.9 As7

The condition of Sudanese cotton and the role of the Colonial Cotton Association.

Extracts from a report submitted by M.F. Lavit at the first Sudan conference of technical and colonial agriculture.

Cotton. Farm Jour. 61(4):15. April 1937.
(Published at Washington Square, Philadelphia, Pa.)   6 F2212

"March plantings of around 15,000 acres in Florida and intentions to plant several thousand acres in Georgia and South Carolina indicate the revival of Sea Island cotton production in the Southeast."

Fleming, Lamar, jr.   Factors affecting U.S. cotton exports.   Cotton Trade Jour. 17(10): 1,2, table. Mar.6,1937. (Published at 810 Union St., New Orleans, La.)   72.8 C8214

To be continued.

Paper read before the Houston Foreign Trade Association. February 26,1937.

Excerpts in Cotton Digest 9(22):4-5,15. Mar.6,1937.

Also in Acco Press 15(3):1-4.   March 1937.

Gturrioz, Rodolfo.   Mexican cotton. Government of Mexico intent on increasing production and aiding the cotton farmer.   Cotton Digest 9(25):6. Mar.27,1937. (Published at 710 Cotton Exchange Bldg., Houston, Tex.) 286.82 C822

Address at Texas Cotton Association Convention held at Galveston, March 19-20.

Harrison, Hubert M.   Cotton improvement work of East Texas chamber of commerce. Cotton Trade Jour. 17(12):4. Mar.20,1937. (Published at 810 Union St., New Orleans, La.) 72.8 C8214

"Address...before the Texas Cotton Association at Galveston," March 19, 1937.

Also in Cotton Digest 9(24):11-14. Mar. 20,1937.

Kitamura, Bunjo. O algodao brasileiro no mercado de algodao mundial. Revista Algodoeira 2(16):15. January 1937. (Published at Recife, Brazil) 72.8 R32
   Brazilian cotton on the world cotton market.

Lanham, W.B., Harper, F.H., and Dodson, Marquerite. Quality of cotton ginned in Mississippi, crops of 1928-34. 38pp., tables, charts, mimeogr. Washington, United States Bureau of agricultural economics, 1937.

Ochoa, R.H. La región algodonera de Antioquia. Boletin Agricola 9(221):784-788. December 1936. (Published at Medellin, Colombia) 9.4 Sol
   The cotton region of Antioquia.

Ousley, Clarence. Value for staple cotton. Acco Press 15(3):6. March 1937. (Published by Anderson, Clayton & Co., Houston, Tex.) 6 Ac2
   From Cotton and Cotton Oil Press.

Pendleton, W.F. Texas quality improvements. Unless program is adopted to better planting seed Texas will lose more markets. Cotton Digest 9(25):5,14. Mar.27,1937. (Published at 710 Cotton Exchange Bldg., Houston, Tex.) 286.82 C822
   Address at meeting of Texas Cotton Association "Better Seed Meeting", Galveston, Texas, March 19,1937.

Sands, W.N. The sea island cotton industry; its progress in the West Indies. West India Com. Circ. 52(1003):83-84. Mar.11, 1937. (Published at 14, Trinity Square, London, E.C.3, England) 8 W524
   To be concluded.

The sea island cotton industry. West India Com. Circ. 52(1003):81. Mar.11,1937. (Published at 14, Trinity Square, London, E.C.3, England) 8 W524
   Editorial on article by W.N. Sands.

Smith, H. Gerald. Cotton trends in Latin
America. Com. Pan Amer. no.56, pp.1-17,
mimeogr. January 1937. (Published by
Pan American Union, Washington, D.C.)

Texas cotton association plans better seed
meeting. Cotton Trade Jour. 17(13):1.
Mar.27,1937. (Published at 810 Union St.,
New Orleans, La.) 72.8 C8214
   Brief report of meeting in Galveston,
March 19 and 20, 1937.

[Tissot, P.] Extension de la culture du coton
dans le Sind. Revue de Botanique Appliquée
et d'Agriculture Tropicale 12(137):927-928.
November 1936. (Published at 57, Rue Cuvier,
Paris (V^e) France) 26 R323
   Expansion of cotton culture in Sind.

Torn, Elmore H. Texas cotton problems. Future
of cotton industry lies in creation of new
uses and improvement of staple. Cotton
Digest 9(21):6-7,14-15. Feb.27,1937.
(Published at 710 Cotton Exchange Bldg.,
Houston, Tex.) 286.82 C822
   "Address given before Dallas Agriculture
Club, February 22," 1937.

Trends in staple length of foreign cotton.
Amer. Ginner and Cotton Oil Miller 14(6):
11-12. February 1937. (Published at P.O.
Box 504, Little Rock, Ark.) 72.8 Am35
   From a summary furnished by the U.S.
Bureau of Agricultural Economics.

United States Bureau of agricultural economics.
Grade, staple length, and tenderability of
cotton in the United States, 1928-29 to
1934-35. U.S. Dept. Agr., Statis. Bull.
56, 63pp., tables, charts. Washington.
1937. 1 Ag84St

20,1937; Cotton Ginners' Jour. 8(7):31-32, 34. April 1937.

Prices

The cotton price outlook. Short-term and long-term contrast. Manchester Guardian Com. 34(868):119,122. Feb.5,1937. (Published at Guardian Bldg., 3 Cross St., Manchester, 2, England)   286.8 M315

Fenner, Charles. Absorption of world's surplus stocks foundation for cotton price upheaval. Cotton Trade Jour. 17(12):7. Mar.20,1937. (Published at 810 Union St., New Orleans, La.)   72.8 C8214
    The reasons for the present rise in cotton prices are discussed.

Hedges, Trimble R. The New York price of American cotton is closely related to prices at other futures exchanges. Okla. Agr. Expt. Sta. Current Farm Econ. Ser.49, 10(1):7-13, tables, chart. February 1937. (Published by the Department of Agricultural Economics, Oklahoma A. & M. College, Stillwater, Okla.)   100 Ok4

Inflation reaches cotton; a dialogue between spinner, manufacturer, and editor Slater. Textile Weekly 19(471):334-335, tables, chart. Mar.12,1937. (Published at 49, Deansgate, Manchester, 3, England)   304.8 T3127
    The present price situation and future possibilities are discussed.

Kapadia, D.F. Cotton prices in relation to quality and yield. Sankhya; Indian Jour. Statis. 2(4):449-452. December 1936. (Published by Karunabindu Biswas, 117-1 Bowbazar St., Calcutta, India)   251.8 In2
    The author replies to a criticism of his paper on "A statistical study of cotton prices in relation to quality and yield," by Prof. P.C. Mahalanobis.

Koshal, R.S. A note on cotton prices in relation to quality and yield. Sankhya; Indian Jour. Statis. 2(4):443-448, tables, charts. December 1936. (Published by Karunabindu

Biswas, 117-1 Bowbazar St., Calcutta, India) 251.8 In2

The author contributes to a discussion between D.F. Kapadia and P.C. Mahalanobis on the subject.

Mann, A.J. Spot cotton prices rise on "squeeze" in March contracts. Com. and Finance 26(5): 178-179. Mar.6,1937. (Published by Comfine Publishing Corp., 95 Broad St., New York, N.Y.) 286.8 C737

The current price situation is described.

Newburger, E. Kirby. The bull market in cotton. Can it be real, and if so--Why? Cotton Trade Jour. 17(12):1,7. Mar.20,1937. (Published at 810 Union St., New Orleans, La.) 72.8 C8214

Sec. Wallace warns against 20-cent cotton "delusion". Cotton Trade Jour. 17(12): 1. Mar.20,1937. (Published at 810 Union St., New Orleans, La.) 72.8 C8214

Prediction by Benjamin Adler of "20-cent cotton next fall" is commented upon.

Marketing and Handling Methods and Practices

Advantages of new contract of New Orleans cotton exchange. Cotton Trade Jour. 17(9):1. Feb. 27,1937. (Published at 810 Union St., New Orleans, La.) 72.8 C8214

Conversion contracts restored by New York cotton exchange. Cotton Trade Jour. 17(13):1. Mar.27,1937. (Published at 810 Union St., New Orleans, La.) 72.8 C8214

"Hog-round" buying. Cotton Digest 9(25):3-4. Mar.27,1937. (Published at 710 Cotton Exchange Bldg., Houston, Tex.) 286.82 C822

Editorial calling the practice "unethical".

It can be done! Acco Press 15(3):7. March 1937. (Published by Anderson, Clayton & Co., Houston, Tex.) 6 Ac2

From Cotton and Cotton Oil Press.

Report of a gin that buys cotton on grade and staple.

"Pioneer". Hog-round buying. Cotton Ginners' Jour. 8(7):42. April 1937. (Published by Texas Cotton Ginners' Association, Inc., 109 North Second Ave., Dallas, Tex.) 304.8 C824

    The experiences of a buyer who bought on grade and staple are given.

Prichard, W.M. Speaking of evils. Cotton Ginners' Jour. 8(7):21-22. April 1937. (Published by Texas Cotton Ginners' Association, Inc., 109 North Second Ave., Dallas, Tex.) 304.8 C824

    The author comments on the suggestion that ginners be prohibited from buying cotton.

Russell, A.L. Contract markets for commodities. 120pp., tables. New York, [1936] 284 R91

    Cotton, pp.40-48; Cottonseed oil, pp.91-94, 112; Cottonseed meal, pp.107-108; London cottonseed, p.112. Customs in various markets and definitions of terms are given.

Thompson, John C. "Hog 'round basis" of buying lowers quality. Cotton Trade Jour. 17(12):5. Mar.20,1937. (Published at 810 Union St., New Orleans, La.) 72.8 C8214

    Address before the Texas Cotton Association at Galveston, March 19, 1937.

    The author comments on the quality of Texas cotton.

Services and Facilities

Burr, C.H. Government policies detrimental to best interests of cotton producers and cotton trade. Cotton Digest 9(24):10, 32-34, table. Mar.20,1937. (Published at 710 Cotton Exchange Bldg., Houston, Tex.) 286.82 C822

    "Sale of Government loan cotton has unquestionably been more successful than was expected by the trade at the time the terms of release were announced just prior to February 1. It seems probable that nearly a million bales will have been released to farmer-producers, when the term of release expires on April 1."

Cotton study courses planned. Cotton Ginners'
Jour. 8(6):9,22. March 1937. (Published
by Texas Cotton Ginners' Association, Inc.,
109 North Second Ave., Dallas, Tex.) 304.8
C824
  Cotton study courses to be given at Texas
A. and M. College, Texas Technological College, and by Anderson, Clayton and Co., for
the purpose of teaching the buying and selling of cotton according to its grade and
staple value are proposed.

Financing of credit purchases. Italian imports
of raw cotton being financed by U.S. bankers.
German barter possibilities. Increase in
supply of "free" cotton as result of CCC
loan cotton release.. Cotton Trade Jour.
17(10):1. Mar.6,1937. (Published at 810
Union St., New Orleans, La.) 72.8 C8214
  Extracts from a report on the cotton
situation by the United States Bureau of
Agricultural Economics are quoted.

McKellar investigates. Cotton Digest 9(24):
17-18. Mar.20,1937. (Published at 710
Cotton Exchange Bldg., Houston, Tex.) 286.82
C822
  A statement received by Senator Kenneth
McKellar regarding government loans to cotton
cooperative associations is commented upon.

Mississippi State college. Cotton marketing
school. [Addresses] delivered before the
cotton marketing school, Mississippi State
College, State College, Mississippi...1936.
[52] pp., mimeogr. [State College, Miss.,
1936] 280.372 M69A
  Contents: Compression and concentration,
by T.R. Spedden; Warehouse and insurance,
by T.R. Spedden; Transportation of cotton,
pt.1-2, by Frank C. Philips.

New Orleans. Board of commissioners. Fortieth
report of the Board of commissioners of the
port of New Orleans...as of June 30, 1936.
48pp., illus., tables. New Orleans, 1936.
286 N47R
  Public cotton warehouse, pp.20-23.

Protest uncertainty in loan cotton sale...Spot merchants' association seeks separation of weight from grade and staple. Cotton Trade Jour. 17(9):1, Feb.27,1937. (Published at 810 Union St., New Orleans, La.) 72.8 C8214
The New Orleans Spot Cotton Merchants' Association has protested to the Commodity Credit Corporation against the uncertainty over possible changes in the terms of the loan cotton sales.

Tariff and loan stocks. Cotton Digest 9(21): 3-4. Feb.27,1937. (Published at 710 Cotton Exchange Bldg., Houston, Tex.) 286.82 C822
Editorial regarding the Government's effort to dispose of stocks of cotton acquired under the loans.

Thornton, E.H. Transit privileges and other advantages of the New Orleans cotton market. Cotton Trade Jour. 17(12):5. Mar.20,1937. (Published at 810 Union St., New Orleans, La.) 72.8 C8214

Marketing Costs

Tu, S.C. Cost of marketing agricultural products along the Nanking-Shanghai-Hangchow railway--Rice, cotton, silk, and silkworm cocoons. China, Min. Indus. Natl. Agr. Research Bur., Spec. Pub.9, 44pp., tables. Nanking. 1935. 22.5 C445S
In Chinese. Summary in English.
"The present study...attempts to analyze the factors affecting market price and to compare the cost of transportation by railway, highway, and waterway."

Cooperation in Marketing

American institute of cooperation. American cooperation, 1936; a collection of papers and discussions comprising the twelfth Summer session...at the University of Illinois, June 15-19, 1936. 750pp., tables. Washington, 1936. 280.29 Am3A
Cooperative marketing of cotton, by N.C. Williamson, pp.21-24.

Annual membership meeting of STCCA held at Corpus Christi. Tex. Co-op. News 17(3): 1. Mar.15,1937. (Published by Texas Co-operative Publishing Co., Inc., 601 Taylor St., Fort Worth, Tex.) 72.9 T315F
    Brief report of annual meeting of South Texas Cotton Cooperative Association, February 23,1937.

Co-op under-classing costly to S.C. farmers. Commissioner of agriculture J. Roy Jones flays ACCA and affiliates after thorough investigation...Recommendations to S.C. legislature seek to curb dangerous practices which may mean loss of millions to cotton South. Cotton Trade Jour. 17(10):1,4. Mar.6,1937. (Published at 810 Union St., New Orleans, La.) 72.8 C8214
    The report to the South Carolina legislature is summarized.
    Also in Cotton Digest 9(22):7,14. Mar.6, 1937.

Cooperativa algodoeira de Joao Pessoa. Brazil. Secretaria de Agricultura, Directoria de Fomento da Produccao Vegetal e de Pesquizas Agronomicas Boletim 2(7/8/9):37-40, illus. July/August/September 1936. 9.2 P2121 (Published at Parahyba, Brazil)
    Cotton cooperative of Joao Pessoa.

Herrmann, O.W. Cooperative cotton marketing in the United States. Pan American union. Div. agr. cooperation. Ser. on cooperatives 3, 32pp. mimeogr. Washington, D.C. 1936. 150.9 C78
    History of the development of cooperative marketing of cotton and cottonseed is given.

How "re-purchase pool" works. Carolina Co-op. 15(3):18. March 1937. (Published by the Carolina Co-operator Publishing Co., corner of Fayetteville and Cabarrus Sts., Raleigh, N.C.) 72.8 N81
    The plan of the North Carolina Cotton Growers' Cooperative Association is described.

Robertson, Caffey. Penetrating analysis of co-op methods. Cotton Trade Jour. 17(12):3. Mar.20,1937. (Published at 810 Union St., New Orleans, La.) 72.8 C8214

United States Farm credit administration. Cooperative division. Lecture notes for film strip, FCA no.101. "Co-op cotton moves to market." 20pp., mimeogr. Washington, [1937]

UTILIZATION

General

Clark, Charles H. The value of scientific research to textile manufacturing. Textile Bull. 51(24):14,62-64. Feb.11,1937. (Published by Clark Publishing Co., 118 West Fourth St., Charlotte, N.C.) 304.8 So62

Co-operating for quality. Cotton Digest 9(21):4. Feb.27,1937. (Published at 710 Cotton Exchange Bldg., Houston, Tex.) 286.82 C822
   Editorial commenting upon the address by Dr. A.G. Black at the Southwestern Cotton Research Conference meeting, February 15, at Dallas, on a cotton research program.

Cotton research laboratory. A proposed new instrument to further the use of cotton. Acco Press 15(3):4. March 1937. (Published by Anderson, Clayton & Co., Houston, Tex.) 6 Ac2
   Resolutions adopted by the Southwestern States Cotton Research Laboratory Conference at Dallas, Texas, February 15,1937, are given.

Galloway, Howard P. Precision through laboratory control. Textile World 87(3):130-131, illus. Feb.28,1937. (Published by McGraw-Hill Publishing Co., Inc., 330 West 42d St., New York, N.Y.) 304.8 T315
   The author discusses the development of laboratories in textile mills.

Hess, Katharine Paddock. Textile fibers and their use. Ed.2, rev. 374pp., illus., tables, charts. Chicago, J.B. Lippincott Co., [1936]

Partial contents: How fabrics are constructed, pp.3-52; How yarn is constructed, pp.53-71; How finishing makes cloth salable, pp.72-85; How colors are applied to textiles, pp.86-100; Textile fibers, their classification and essential properties, pp.119-129; Cotton: its importance and use, pp.190-221; Factors influencing textile consumption, pp.267-284; How to select fabrics for clothing and household use, pp.285-332; and The care of fabrics, pp.333-362.

Schwarz, E.R. Precision through research. Textile World 87(3):128, illus. Feb.28,1937. (Published by McGraw-Hill Publishing Co., Inc., 330 West 42d St., New York, N.Y.) 304.8 T315

The author discusses the need for research in the textile industry.

Fiber, Yarn, and Fabric Quality.

Bonner, J. Zum mechanismus der zellstreckung auf grund der micellarlehre. Jahrbücher für Wissenschaftliche Botanik 82(3):377-412. 1935. (Published at Leipzig, Germany) 450 P93J

The mechanism of cell stretching on the basis of the micellar theory.

"According to the author's conception of the micellar structure of the young parenchymatous cell wall, the cellulose framework must be responsible for the mechanical and optical properties of the wall and the young cell wall must be thought of as 'living'. In artificial stretching the micellar framework of the cell walls (parenchymatous and epidermal) behaves like that of artificial cellulose products, such as Cellophane and synthetic silk. Since the orientating effect of the cell wall micelles is partly or completely absent in growth, the latter must be considered as a simple, plastic stretching." - Expt. Sta. Rec.75(2):184. August 1936.

Chevenard, Pierre. Très petite machine de traction à enregistrement photographique et son application à l'étude des fibres textiles. Académie des Sciences, Comptes Rendus Hebdomadaires des Séances 203(18):

841-843, charts. Nov.3,1936. (Published at Quai des Grands-Augustins 55, Paris, France) 505 P21
Very small instrument for photographic recording and its application to the study of textile fibers.
"A device is briefly described which is capable of tracing load-extension diagrams with fibres of 1 to 10 mm. length, the breaking load of which is no more than 0.02 gram. Typical diagrams are reproduced for rayon, silk, wool, ramie and camel's hair."-Textile Inst. Jour. 28(1):A36. January 1937.

Cleveland, Richard S. Calibration of a "constant rate of loading" machine for testing the tensile properties of textiles. Rayon Textile Mo. 18(3):75-76, table, chart. March 1937. (Published at 303 Fifth Ave., New York, N.Y.) 304.8 R21
"The data given in this paper were presented orally before Subcommittee B1 Section 3 on machines, Committee D13, A.S.T.M., October 1935."

Davidson, G.F.. The dissolution of chemically modified cotton cellulose in alkaline solutions. Part 3--In solutions of sodium and potassium hydroxide containing dissolved zinc, beryllium and aluminium oxides. Textile Inst. Jour. 28(2):T27-T44, tables, charts. February 1937. (Published at 16 St. Mary's Parsonage, Manchester, 3, England) 73.9 T31
References, p.T44.

[Edelstein, Sidney M.] Study and control of mercerization. Methods used in experimental laboratory--Skein mercerizing machine--Yarn is neutralized, washed and dried--Dye affinity and luster determinations. Amer. Wool & Cotton Reptr. 51(10):15,22. Mar.11,1937. (Published by Frank P. Bennett & Co., Inc., 530 Atlantic Ave., Boston, Mass.) 304.8 W88

Grimes, Mary Anna. The effect of exposure in the field on grade, strength, and color of raw cotton. Tex. Agr. Expt. Sta. Bull.538, 35pp., tables, charts. College Station, 1936. 100 T31B
Literature cited, p.35.
"From this study it is concluded that to

obtain a product of high quality in grade, strength, and color, commanding the best price, cotton should be harvested not later than four or five weeks, and preferably within the first one or two weeks, after opening."

Guernsey, F.H., and Howells, L.T. The evaluation of chemical tendering of cellulose by cellulose viscosity measurement. Amer. Dyestuff Reptr. 26(3):P62-P67, illus., chart. Feb.8,1937. (Published by Howes Publishing Co., Inc., 440 Fourth Ave., New York, N.Y.) 306.8 Am3

References, p.P66.

Paper presented at annual meeting of American Association of Textile Chemists and Colorists, Providence, R.I., Dec.5,1936.

The authors conclude that "this method has almost unlimited possibilities in the determination and control of chemical tendering in cotton fabric, and, therefore, serves as a criterion in judging the chemical resistance of new merchandise."

Hardy, Arthur C. The applicability of spectrophotometry to the solution of color problems in the textile industry. Amer. Dyestuff Reptr. 26(3):P67-P71, charts. Feb. 8,1937. (Published by Howes Publishing Co., Inc., 440 Fourth Ave., New York, N.Y.) 306.8 Am3

Paper presented at the annual meeting of the American Association of Textile Chemists and Colorists, Providence, R.I., December 5, 1936.

Hess, Kurt, Trogus, Carl, and Vergin, Wilhelm. Untersuchungen über die bildung der pflanzlichen zellwand. Planta 25(3):419-437, illus., tables, charts. June 18,1936. (Published by Julius Springer, Linkstrasse 22/24, Berlin, W9, Germany) 450 P693

Study of the structure of the plant cell wall.

"With the aid of X-ray methods, two easily distinguishable crystalline constituents can be detected in growing cotton hairs. The one is only present during cell elongation, and is called the primary substance. The other first appears after completion of elongation, that is, at the beginning of the secondary thickening of the cell-wall. This is the crystalline form of cellulose, which is confirmed by micro-chemical and optical data. The conclusion is drawn that crystalline cellulose is not present during the lengthening phase; amorphous cellulose may be present."-Textile Inst. Jour. 28(1):A35. January 1937.

Huzino, Kiyohisa. Relation between fiber length and yarn twist affecting the strength of the cotton yarn. Rayon Textile Mo. 18 (1):104. January 1937. (Published at 303 Fifth Ave., New York, N.Y.) 304.8 R21

From J. Soc. Text. Ind., p.363. Japan. 1936.

"When a spun yarn is broken, it will be seen at the breaking section that some fibers break off and the others slip off. Equations have been introduced representing the functional relation among fiber-length, fiber-thickness, fiber-strength, friction coefficient of fiber and yarn twist, and determined the condition of the breaking-off or the slipping-off of the fibers. It was found in conclusion, in relation to the fiber-length and yarn twist which are the most important factors for spinning, that the strength of cotton yarn is not influenced."

Kurtz, Friedrich. Ein neuer festigkeitsprüfer für einzelfasern nach dem prinzip des Deforden. Melliand Textilberichte 17(10):781-783, illus., table, charts. October 1936. (Published at Heidelberg, Germany) 304.8 T312

A new strength tester for single fibers after the principle of Deforden.

"A detailed description is given of a new strength tester for single fibres which is of the balance type and constructed on the same principles as the Deforden testing apparatus. Its use for breaking load and extension determinations is illustrated by a study of tests on viscose staple fibre. The use of the apparatus for investigations of elasticity is discussed."-Textile Inst. Jour. 28(1):A36. January 1937.

Macormac, A.R., and Cameron, F.K. Pulps from the whole cotton plant; comparison of soda

and nitric acid pulps. Indus. and Engin. Chem. 29(1):96-97. January 1937. (Published by American Chemical Society, Mills Bldg., Washington, D.C.) 381 J825
    Literature cited, p.97.

Meyer, Kurt H., and Lotmar, Walter. Sur l'élasticité de la cellulose. IV. Sur la constitution de la partie cristallisée de la cellulose. Helvetica Chimica Acta 19(1):68-86, tables, charts. Feb.15,1936. (Published by Georg & Co., Basel, Switzerland) 385 H36
    The elasticity of cellulose. IV. The constitution of the crystallized cellulose portion.

    "Investigations were made to show the effect of moisture, temp., orientation and tension on the modulus of elasticity of cellulose and its derivs. (artificial silk, Cellophane, etc.). A positive coeff. of heat, characteristic of rubber, is found only with cellulose acetate. In the other cases the coeffs. are zero or neg. and the mechanism of the elasticity varies considerably from that of rubber. Valence forces of the mol. are responsible for the elasticity. The modulus of elasticity of native fibers (ramie, hemp, and linen) which are well oriented is approx. 11,000 kg. per sq. mm. With the derivs. of cellulose, the modulus of elasticity is lower (100-5000 kg. per sq. mm.). This is due to the fact that the fiber structure is not regular; there are spaces between the crystallites which prevent a simple relationship between the modulus of elasticity and their constitution."- Chem. Abs. 30(22):8601-8602. Nov.20,1936.

Odintzov, P.N., Tsuipkina, M.N., and Ergorova, L.V. The components of the cotton husk and their chemical properties. Chem. Abs. 30(16): 5611-5612. Aug. 20,1936. (Published by American Chemical Society, Mills Bldg., Washington, D.C.)
    From Jour. Applied Chem. (U.S.S.R.)9:119-138. 1936.

    The method of successive definitive extns. can be successfully employed in the study of plant materials making possible a sepn. into homogeneous fractions. It also permits observation of the physical and chem. changes

occurring in the solid material during extn.
The cotton husks, previously extd. with Et_2O
and EtOH, were extd. repeatedly at 50° with
H_2O for the removal of sugars, tannins
and other readily sol. substances, then successively with H_2O at 100° and in an auto-
clave at 120°, in all 61 sep. extns. with
H_2O. The husks exhausted with H_2O were then
boiled successively with aq. and alc. NaOh.
Lignin joins the epidermis to the other layers
of the cells, pectins and sol. lignin the
interior layer to the remainder. There was
very little actual tannin in the husks, which
are therefore unsuitable for use in tanning.
The resin or substance X of the literature is
probably intermediate in compn. between tannin
and lignin."

Pearson, Norma L. Naps, neps, motes, and seed-
coat fragments; a description of certain ele-
ments of cotton quality. 7pp., illus.,
processed. Washington, D.C., U.S. Department
of Agriculture, Bureau of Agricultural Economics,
1937

Rath, Hermann, ter Kuile, and Jäger. Zur frage
der merzerisation von mischgespinsten aus
baumwolle/zellwolle. Zeitschrift für die
Gesamte Textil-Industrie 39(35):493-497, charts.
Aug. 26, 1936. (Published by L.A. Klepzig,
Leipzig, C 1, Germany)
    The problem of the mercerization of
mixed textile fabrics from cotton and spun
rayon.

Riso, Raffaele, and Levi, Camillo. Caratteris-
tiche di alcuni cotoni nazionali. Bolettino
della Cotoniera 31(12):596-608, illus., tables,
charts. December 1936. (Published at Via
Borgonuovo, 11, Milano, Italy)   304.8 B63
    Characteristics of some national cottons.

Scroggie, Arthur G., and Castricum, Martin.
Incline plane yarn testing. Importance of
uniformity in the constant rate of loading.
Textile Research 7(5):211-212, table. March
1937. (Published by United States Institute
for Textile Research, 65 Franklin St., Boston,
Mass.)   304.8 T293
    "For convenience in comparing the cotton

values indicated, with similar properties of rayon yarns, the table includes the denier value corresponding to the cotton count and the tensile strength in grams per denier. These values are comparable to those printed in Dr. Hunter's article referred to."

Sokurova-Vysotskaia, O. [Measurements of the lint length of cotton under field conditions. An apparatus constructed by the Central breeding station, NIHI.] Bor'ba za Khlopok, no. 8/9, pp.127-132, illus., tables. August/September 1935. (Published at Tashkent, U.S.S.R.) 72.8 B64
In Russian.

"A cheap and simple device costing 1-15 roubles is described whereby measurements of lint can be made with deviations of not more than 1 mm. from measurements with Palls' apparatus. By its aid measurements on 500 seeds can be made and entered in the field during an 8-hour day by an unskilled worker."-Empire Cotton Growing Rev. 13(3):233. July 1936.

Sommer, H. Zusammendrückbarkeit und weichheit von textilien. Melliand Textilberichte 17 (8,9,10):630-632, 712-714, 786-788, illus., tables, charts. August, September, October 1936. (Published at Heidelberg, Germany) 304.8 T312
Compressibility and softness of textiles.

"Various methods for the determination of the compressibility and softness of fibres, yarns and fabrics are described and typical results are given and discussed. The determinations are based on measurements of the change in form produced by pressure. The change in area of cross-section of yarn or in thickness of fabric produced by a tenfold change in pressure is the absolute measure of softness and its relative value expressed as a percentage gives the compressibility. Standard thicknesses are measured under a pressure of 10g./sq. cm. and these values are used in determinations of apparent specific weight and compressibility is discussed."-Textile Inst. Jour. 28(1):A35. January 1937.

Strength of cotton and rayon cords. Amer. Wool & Cotton Reptr. 51(10):45-46. Mar.11,1937. (Published by Frank P. Bennett & Co., Inc., 530 Atlantic Ave., Boston, Mass.) 304.8 W88
 A reply to a letter regarding the comparative strength of cotton and rayon cords for tires.

Technology of Manufacture

About spinning travelers. Some interesting facts furnished by the leading American traveler manufacturers as well as data gleaned from other sources. Saco-Lowell Bull. 9(1):1-11, illus., tables, charts. February 1937. (Published at 147 Milk St., Boston, Mass.) 304.8 Sa1

B., C. Ring spinning--XI. Importance of high quality in spinning rings--The best procedure in regard to lubricating the rings--Testing of ring plates--Oiling the spindles, frequency, removal of dirty oil, oil quality--Driving the spindles--Re-banding. Textile Mercury and Argus 96(2498):132,133, illus. Feb.5, 1937. (Published at 41, Spring Gardens, Manchester, England) 304.8 T318

Belshaw, R. Controversies in cotton spinning. Textile Manfr. 62(744):461. December 1936. (Published by Emmott & Co., Ltd. 31 King St., West, Manchester, 3, England) 304.8 T3126
 Report of a lecture to the Manchester College of Technology Textile Society, November 17, 1936.
 High-drafting, single process lapping, high-speed winding and beaming, warping from ring bobbins, "broken-back" ring frame roller stands, and diameter and lift of ring bobbins, are discussed.

The card cylinder. Some facts regarding the design, care, and functions of this essential part of the card machine. Saco-Lowell Bull. 9(1):22-26, illus., tables. February 1937. (Published at 147 Milk St., Boston, Mass.) 304.8 Sa1

Cotton card clothing and stripping. A new method of reducing the work of stripping

of cards. Textile Manfr. 62(741):330. September 1936. (Published by Emmott & Co., Ltd., 31 King St., West, Manchester, 3,England). 304.8 T3126
"A new method, the Baumann 'Reform' card is mentioned by Dr. Stoll in 'Melliand', July, 1936, p.551."

Hodge, William B. Textile industry pioneered in air conditioning. Textile Bull. 51(24): 20,64-66, illus. Feb.11,1937. (Published by Clark Publishing Co., 118 West Fourth St., Charlotte, N.C.) 304.8 So82

Hunt, W.A. Waste can sink profits in a cotton mill. Textile World 87(4):728-729, illus. March 1937. (Published by McGraw-Hill Publishing Co., Inc., 330 West 42d St., New York, N.Y.) 304.8 T315

Landau, A.K. Modern machines and methods establish new standards. Textile Bull. 51(24):26,59. Feb.11,1937. (Published by Clark Publishing Co., 118 West Fourth St., Charlotte, N.C.) 304.8 So82
New machines and methods for opening, carding, drawing and spinning are described.

Merrill, Gilbert R. Getting the mill in balance on print cloth. Textile World 87(4): 741, table. March 1937. (Published by McGraw-Hill Publishing Co., Inc., 330 West 42d St., New York, N.Y.) 304.8 T315
"This print-cloth mill is taken as an illustration of a complete layout to produce gray cloth."

The 1926 vs. 1936 mill. A comparison of two modern plants built only ten years apart. Saco-Lowell Bull. 9(1):15-19, tables, charts. February 1937. (Published at 147 Milk St., Boston, Mass.) 304.8 Sa1

Oversby, R.G. Textile alignment charts--III. Applications of alignment charts or nomograms in the setting of cloths and cloth building. Textile Manfr. 63(745):14-16, charts. January 1937. (Published by Emmott & Co., Ltd., 31 King St., West, Manchester,3, England) 304.8 T3126

Platt Brothers and Co. Ltd. High-draft cotton ring spinning. Conversion of ring frames from three roller lines system to four lines high-draft system. Textile Manfr. 63(745): 20,26,illus. January 1937. (Published by Emmott & Co., Ltd., 31 King St., West, Manchester, 3, England) 304.8 T3126

Pratt, Horace L. A million more long draft spinning spindles, with continued development of long-draft roving--Other advances. Textile World 87(3):142-143, illus. Feb.28, 1937. (Published by McGraw-Hill Publishing Co., Inc., 330 West 42d St. New York, N.Y.) 304.8 T315

Reducing spinning costs. The "Dawes" system. Textile Weekly 19(472):368, illus. Mar.19, 1937. (Published at 49, Deansgate, Manchester, 3, England) 304.8 T3127

Regularity in cotton drafting. Textile Manfr. 63(745):24, illus. January 1937. (Published by Emmott & Co., Ltd., 31 King St., West, Manchester, 3, England) 304.8 T3126
"A patented loose-boss roller has an inner sleeve which may tilt on a middle ball-like part of the arbour. Yarn faults due to eccentricity of shells or coverings are thereby avoided."

Roving goes long draft. Change to single process promises to hold spotlight as outstanding trend of 1937 in cotton manufacture. Textile World 87(4):722-723, illus., table. March 1937. (Published by McGraw-Hill Publishing Co., Inc., 330 West 42d St., New York, N.Y.) 304.8 T315

Technology of Consumption

Goodyear offers rayon cord tires for heavy duty use. Results of 10 years of experiments-- For trucks and buses--Will outwear other types is claim. Daily News Rec. no.49, pp.1,15. Mar.1,1937. (Published at 8 East 13th St., New York, N.Y.) 286.8 N48

McConnell, R.J.   Past 15 years have witnessed
   many major improvements. Textile Bull.
   51(24):18,67-68. Feb.11,1937. (Published
   by Clark Publishing Co., 118 West Fourth St.,
   Charlotte, N.C.)   304.8 So82
      Developments in textile machinery are
   described.

Nutty business. California walnut growers assn.
   builds new storage using damp muslin as cool-
   ing agent. Power Plant Engin. 40(11):646-
   647, illus. November 1936. (Published by
   Technical Publishing Co., 53 W. Jackson Blvd.,
   Chicago, Ill.)   290.8 P88

O'Brien, R., and Hays, M.B.   Sheets again.
   Jour. Home Econ. 29(1):11-15. January 1937,
   (Published by the American Home Economics
   Association, Mills Bldg., Washington, D.C.)
   321.8 J82
      Suggestions for standards for the construc-
   tion of sheeting are given.

Technology of shrinkage dissected at FTC parley.
   Daily News Rec. no.57, pp.1,20. Mar.10,1937.
   (Published at 8 East 13th St., New York, N.Y.)
   286.8 N48
      "The Federal Trade Commission's hearing on
   the proposed shrinkage rules for woven cotton
   yard goods, held yesterday at the Hotel Astor
   before Commissioner Miller, was every bit as
   interesting as had been anticipated...Recon-
   oiling technical and mechanical irregulari-
   ties and uncertainties with consumer ambitions,
   was one phase of yesterday's discussions.
   Another phase was the disagreement, of some
   mills with finishing plants, with the job
   finishers."
      Also in Fibre and Fabric 90(2719):6-7.
   Mar.13,1937.

Whitcomb, William H.   Precision through standard
   specifications. Textile World 87(3):129,
   illus. Feb.28,1937. (Published by McGraw-
   Hill Publishing Co., Inc., 330 West 42d St.,
   New York, N.Y.)   304.8 T315
      The need for standard specifications for
   cloth constructions is discussed.

COTTONSEED AND COTTONSEED PRODUCTS

[Childress, G.L.] Cottonseed oil refining.
Oil Mill Gazetteer 41(9):17-19. March 1937.
(Published at Wharton, Tex.) 307.8 Oi53
"This paper was read before the juniors
and seniors of the chemical engineering
division, Texas A. and M. College, College
Station."

Does staple length of cotton affect the value
of seed from a milling standpoint? Cotton
and Cotton Oil Press 38(11):7. Mar. 13,
1937. (Published at 3116-18 Commerce St.,
Dallas, Tex.) 304.8 C822
Opinions of several persons are given.

Great Britain. Imperial economic committee.
Intelligence branch. Vegetable oils and
oil seeds; a summary of figures of production
and trade relating to cottonseed, linseed,
rapeseed, sesame seed, soya beans, ground
nuts, copra, palm kernels, palm oil and olive
oil. 89pp. London, H.M. Stationery off.,
1936. (Gt. Brit. Imperial economic committee.
Intelligence branch. [I.E.C./C.8, November]
1936) 280.39 G794C
Cottonseed (production, exports, imports,
prices), pp. 10-19.

Labor and the oil mills. Cotton and Cotton
Oil Press 38(10):15. Mar. 6, 1937. (Published at 3116-18 Commerce St., Dallas,
Tex.) 304.8 C822
Cottonseed oil mills "who are guilty of
this low-wage practice, can find the solution if they diligently seek it."

Lehnberg, Werner. Cotton oil's inherent
strength. Com. and Finance 26(6):196,
table. Mar. 20, 1937. (Published by Comfine Publishing Corp., 95 Broad St., New
York, N.Y.) 286.8 C737
The present market situation is analyzed.

National cottonseed products association, inc.
Cottonseed and its products, an actual and
potential source of wealth of national importance. 34pp., illus., tables, charts. Memphis, 1937.
Revision of a pamphlet entitled "Facts
about a great exclusively southern industry."

Olcott, H.S., and Mattill, H.A.. Antioxidants and the autoxidation of fats. VII. Preliminary classification of inhibitors. Amer. Chem. Soc. Jour. 58(11):2204-2208, tables. November 1936. (Published at Mills Bldg., Washington, D.C.) 381 Am33J
"Presented before the Division of Agricultural and Food Chemistry at the 92nd meeting of the American Chemical Society, Pittsburgh, Pa., September 7 to 11, 1936."
Cottonseed oil was used in the experiments.

Seed grading in Mississippi. Cotton and Cotton Oil Press 38(11):13. Mar.13,1937. (Published at 3116-18 Commerce St., Dallas, Tex.) 304.8 C822
Comments on the practice during the past six years of purchasing seed on grade are given.

Tanganyika territory, Department of veterinary science and animal husbandry. Annual report... 1935. 155pp., illus., tables, charts. Dar Es Salaam, 1936. 41.9 T15
The value of cotton-seed in the dietary of zebu cattle, by M.H.French, pp.110-116.

Would seed grading protect the grower? Cotton and Cotton Oil Press 38(9):10-11. Feb.27,1937. (Published at 3116-18 Commerce St., Dallas, Tex.) 304.8 C822
A publication by A.M. Dickson entitled, "Cottonseed prices in the United States for Season of 1934-35" is commented upon.

LEGISLATION, REGULATION, AND ADJUDICATION

Antigua. Duty-free importation of certain cotton goods. Gt. Brit. Bd. Trade Jour. 138(2096):174. Feb.4,1937. (Published by H.M. Stationery Office, Adastral House, Kingsway, London, W.C.2, England) 256.03 T67J
Goods made from West Indian Sea Island cotton are exempt from duty.

Bercaw, Louise O. Incidence of the processing taxes under the agricultural adjustment act; a selected list of references. U.S. Dept.

Agr., Bur. Agr. Econ., Agr. Econ. Bibliog.
68, 46pp., mimeogr. Washington, 1937.
1.9 Ec73A
    Cotton, pp.11-22.

Bill favored for laboratory.   Cotton Digest
    9(24):27-28. Mar.20,1937. (Published at
    710 Cotton Exchange Bldg., Houston, Tex.)
    286.82 C822
    A bill introduced in the Texas legislature by George Moffet provides for establishment of a cotton research laboratory in that state.

Brazil (Rio Grande Do Norte).   Cotton--Export
    duty increased and collectible in advance of
    shipment--Export restriction on cotton seed
    authorized. Com. Reports no.13, p.257.
    Mar.27,1937. (Published by U.S. Bureau of
    Foreign and Domestic Commerce, Washington,
    D.C.)   157 C76D

Brazilian State adopts sweeping cotton regulations. Foreign Agr. 1(3):152-153. March
    1937. (Published by Bureau of Agricultural
    Economics, United States Department of Agriculture, Washington, D.C.)
    "The legislature of the state of Rio
    Grande de Norte in northeastern Brazil adopted a law on December 9 which, if strictly
    enforced, will seriously handicap the operations of foreign concerns engaged in the
    ginning, baling, and exporting of cotton,
    according to a report from American Consul
    George J. Haering in Pernambuco." Provisions
    of the law are noted.

British West Africa. Piece-goods of cotton
    and/or artificial silk: Gold coast and
    Nigerian quotas. Indian Trade Jour. 124
    (1595):134. Jan.14,1937. (Published by
    the Department of Commercial Intelligence
    and Statistics, 1, Council House St.,
    Calcutta, India)   286.8 In24
    "During 1937 each foreign country will
    be permitted to import into Nigeria and the
    Gold Coast either the same volume of textile
    goods of the varieties now to be subject to
    quota restriction as it supplied during the
    year 1935 plus 50 per cent or 2 1/2 per cent

of the total imports of such textiles from all sources during 1935, whichever is the greater. There will be one quota for cotton piece-goods and another for artificial silk piece-goods. In the Gold Coast there will also be a separate quota for cotton towels."

Christy, D.F. Trade agreements and the farmer. 12pp., mimeogr. [Washington] United States Bureau of Agricultural Economics 1937
   Address at Cooperative Marketing School, Little Rock, Arkansas, February 26, 1937.
   The effect on the cotton farmer is noted.

Congress activity. Review and outlook of legislation affecting the cotton trade. Cotton Digest 9(24):16-17. Mar.20,1937. (Published at 710 Cotton Exchange Bldg., Houston, Tex.) 286.82 C822
   The status of legislation before the United States Congress is described.

Cotton threatened. Cotton Digest 9(24):19-20. Mar.20,1937. (Published at 710 Cotton Exchange Bldg., Houston, Tex.) 286.82 C822
   "The cotton industry--supplier of one of the most important necessities of war--is seen threatened with a serious set-back at the hands of a minority Congressional bloc if their will to force a mandatory neutrality policy upon the Administration proves successful in the pending neutrality fight...The real threat to cotton comes...from the effect a mandatory neutrality policy would have in encouraging production in other areas."

Gray, Cecil. Farmer opposes Fulmer net weight bill. Cotton Digest 9(21):5. Feb.27,1937. (Published at 710 Cotton Exchange Bldg., Houston, Tex.) 286.82 C822

Netherlands East Indies. Import restriction on unbleached [and bleached] cotton piece-goods. Gt. Brit. Bd. Trade Jour. 138(2095): 145-146. Jan.28,1937. (Published by H.M. Stationery Office, Adastral House, Kingsway, London, W.C.2, England) 256.03 T67J

Ousley, Clarence. The Kleberg bill. Cotton and Cotton Oil Press 38(9):14. Feb.27,1937. (Published at 3116-18 Commerce St., Dallas, Tex.)   304.8 C822
　　The bill "provides for...relaxation of the tax on margarine dealers."

Parker, Walter. The south and its future. Cotton Ginners' Jour. 8(6):13,20. March 1937. (Published by Texas Cotton Ginners' Association, Inc., 109 North Second Ave., Dallas, Tex.)   304.8 C824
　　The author urges removal of tariffs in order to help the South sell its surplus cotton.

[Shumard, F.W.] The anti-price discrimination law. Robinson-Patman law recently passed presents serious problems which industry must meet through better cost records. Cotton Ginners' Jour. 8(6):23-24. March 1937. (Published by Texas Cotton Ginners' Association, Inc., 109 North Second Ave., Dallas, Tex.)   304.8 C824

United States Agricultural adjustment administration. 1937 agricultural conservation program, southern region bulletin 101, amendment 4. Fed. Register 2(40):526-527. Mar. 2,1937. (Published by National Archives, Washington, D.C.)   169 F31
　　Matters which may be appealed and procedure governing appeals from recommendations of the County Committee are given.

United States Agricultural adjustment administration. 1937 agricultural conservation program, southern region bulletin 101, amendment 7. Fed. Register 2(57):679. Mar.25, 1937. (Published by National Archives, Washington, D.C.)   169 F31
　　Regulations for obtaining triple superphosphate at Sheffield, Alabama, are given.

United States Agricultural adjustment administration. 1937 agricultural conservation program, southern region bulletin 101, Kemper county, Mississippi. Fed. Register 2(54):649-654. Mar.20,1937. (Published by National Archives, Washington, D.C.)   169 F31

[United States Interstate commerce commission]
Cotton adjustment revised. Traffic World
59(11):537-538. Mar.13,1937. (Published
at 418 S. Market St., Chicago, Ill.) 288.8
T672
  Freight rate decisions as to cotton yarn
and piece goods in the South are clarified.

[United States Interstate commerce commission]
Proposed reports. Cotton. Traffic World
59(11):541. Mar.13,1937. (Published at
418 S. Market St., Chicago, Ill.) 288.8
T672
  Compressed and uncompressed cotton are
not considered the same for rate-making
purposes.

What some of the people who will "foot the
bill" say about Representative Fulmer's
"cotton bagging" bills. Amer. Ginner
and Cotton Oil Miller 14(6):7-8. February
1937. (Published at P.O. Box 504, Little
Rock, Ark.) 72.8 Am35

Williams, Ben J. Subsidy for cotton South to
offset tariff. Cotton Trade Jour. 17(12):
5. Mar.20,1937. (Published at 810 Union
St., New Orleans, La.) 72.8 C8214
  The author advocates such a subsidy.

[Williamson, N.C.] Net weight and cotton
bagging. Cotton and Cotton Oil Press
38(11):3-4. Mar.13,1937. (Published at
3116-18 Commerce St., Dallas, Tex.)
304.8 C822
  Excerpts from hearings and other comments
in favor of the Fulmer net weight bill are
included.

MISCELLANEOUS-GENERAL

Burrill, Meredith F. A socio-economic atlas
of Oklahoma. 124pp., charts. Stillwater,
1936. 280.069 B94
  Maps show location of cotton acreage and
production, p.34; cotton gins and compresses,
p.90; cottonseed products, p.91; cotton harvested by snapping, p.115,

Cox, A.B. Cotton: Tex. Business Rev. 11(1):
5-6. Feb.27,1937. (Published by Bureau of
Business Research, University of Texas, Austin,
Tex.) 280.8 T312
   The author discusses the need for foreign
markets for American cotton and the proposal
for a laboratory to discover new uses for
cotton.

International institute of agriculture. Bibliography of tropical agriculture, 1935,
256pp. Rome, 1936. 241 In8B
   Textiles--Cotton, pp.149-170.

Lancashire Indian cotton committee. Third
annual report...for the year ended 31st
December 1936. 34pp., illus., tables,
charts. [Manchester, England, Harlequin
Press Co., Ltd., 1937] 286.3729 Ar3
   Includes a brief report of technological
investigations of Indian cottons and a
statement of the future outlook for Indian
cotton in the United Kingdom.
   Abstract in Textile Mercury and Argus
(Suppl.) p.22B. Feb.19,1937; Manchester
Chamber of Com, Mo. Rec. 48(2):76-78. Feb.
28, 1937.

Rostron, H. The training of operatives in
the textile industry. Textile Weekly
19(471):351,353. Mar.12,1937. (Published at 49, Deansgate, Manchester, 3,
England) 304.8 T3127
   "In a lecture to the British Association of Managers of Textile Works, February 27, 1937."

Saklatwala, S.D. Cotton from field to factory.
Poona Agr. Coll. Mag. 28(3):98-107. December
1936. (Published at the Agricultural College,
Poona, India) 22 P79
   Agriculture, history, technology, commerce
and manufacture of Indian cotton are discussed.

South Carolina Agricultural experiment station.
Forty-ninth annual report...for the year
ended June 30,1936. 144pp., illus., tables,
charts. Clemson, 1936. 100 So8
   Partial contents: Grade and staple esti-

mates and cotton marketing study, by Harry A. White, pp.14-15; Variation in cotton fiber length, fineness, and maturity in several varieties, by G.M. Armstrong, C.C. Bennett, and B.S. Hawkins, pp.28-30; The effect of magnesium in the mineral nutrition of the cotton plant, pp.31-33; Cotton seedling diseases by C.H. Arndt, pp.34-38; Cotton insect studies, by J.G. Watts, pp.45-50; Cotton variety test on large plot basis, by C.S. Patrick, p.65; Cotton breeding, by E.D. Kyzer, and W.H. Jenkins, pp.72-73; Cotton production studies, by E.E. Hall and F.M. Harrell, pp.74-79; Boll weevil and miscellaneous cotton insect investigations, by F.F. Bondy and C.F. Rainwater, pp.85-89; Yields of seed cotton from the use of acid and non-acid fertilizers, by H.P. Cooper and R.W. Wallace, pp.107-115; and Fertilizer placement experiments with cotton, by Nelson McKaig, Jr., pp.119-121.

Stokes, W.E. Sea island cotton. Fla. Agr. Expt. Sta,, Press Bull. 500, 2pp. Gainsville, 1937. 100 F66S
    Pure seed necessary, growing, weevil control, handling the crop, community production.

ooOoo

COTTON REPORTS

ISSUED CURRENTLY BY
UNITED STATES GOVERNMENT DEPARTMENTS

U.S. Department of Agriculture, Bureau of A icultural

Cotton Situation: issued monthly.

Crop Reports (Summarized in Crops and Markets, which is issu
to be issued May 21, July 8, Aug. 9, Sept. 8, Oct. 8, Nov
1937.

Grade and Staple Reports:
  Grade, Staple Length and Tenderability of Cotton Ginned i
  States: to be issued Apr. 16, 1937.
  Weekly Grade and Staple Summary: issued Saturdays during
  of ginning season, at Washington.
  Weekly Grade and Staple Reports: issued Saturdays during
  ginning season, at Atlanta, Ga.; Memphis, Tenn.; Dalla
  and El Paso, Tex.

Market News Reports:
  American Cotton Linters Price Report: issued Wednesdays
  D.C.
  Daily Official Report of the Designated Spot Cotton Marke
  Atlanta, Ga.
  Staple Cotton Premiums: issued Saturdays at Atlanta, Ga.
  Tenn., and Dallas, Tex.
  Cotton Market Review: issued Saturdays at Washington, D.
  lanta, Ga., Memphis, Tenn., and Dallas, Tex.

U.S. Department of Commerce, Bureau of the Census

Activity in the Cotton Spinning Industry: issued monthly, a
Cotton Consumed, on Hand, Imported and Exported, and Active
  Spindles: issued monthly, about the 14th.
Cottonseed Received, Crushed, and on Hand, and Cottonseed Pr
  Manufactured, Shipped out, on Hand and Exported: issued
  about the 12th.
Report on Cotton Ginnings: reports on 1937 crop to be issue
  Aug.23, Sept.8, Sept.23, Oct.8, Oct.25, Nov.8, Nov.22, De
  Dec.20, 1937, Jan.24, Mar.21, 1938.

U.S. Department of Commerce, Bureau of Foreign and Domest

Textile Raw Materials: issued weekly.
Textiles and Allied Products: issued weekly.